SpringerBriefs in Digital Spaces

For further volumes:
http://www.springer.com/series/10461

Omar A. El Sawy · Francis Pereira

Business Modelling in the Dynamic Digital Space

An Ecosystem Approach

 Springer

Omar A. El Sawy
Marshall School of Business
University of Southern California
Los Angeles, CA
USA

Francis Pereira
Marshall School of Business
University of Southern California
Los Angeles, CA
USA

ISSN 2193-5890   ISSN 2193-5904   (electronic)
ISBN 978-3-642-31764-4   ISBN 978-3-642-31765-1   (eBook)
DOI 10.1007/978-3-642-31765-1
Springer Heidelberg New York Dordrecht London

Library of Congress Control Number: 2012942917

Printed on acid-free paper

Springer is part of Springer Science+Business Media (www.springer.com)

Foreword

This book is the first in the SpringerBriefs series on Digital Spaces, a joint initiative taken recently by Springer, CIGREF and myself, as editor of the Series. The series aims to provide to the research, business and policy communities, the concepts, ideas and results of projects carried out under Information System Dynamics (ISD) Program, an international research programme initiated in 2009 by the CIGREF Foundation. It is designed to bring together the best expertise available at the international level to focus on the area of public interest that evaluates the societal and managerial challenges in the long-term usage of information systems and "digitality." The ISD programme views the issue of the use of information systems (and digitality) as a societal issue, beyond the scope of just corporations. From this perspective, the programme's objectives are twofold:

- *General objective*: to understand the many facets involved in the dynamic use of information systems over a long period, especially by focusing on emerging factors in different geographical and business contexts;
- *Specific objective*: to provide the stakeholders (large companies, IT providers, government, academics, media) with the analytical tools that will help them to understand the strategic issues arising from the changes under way

In light of these objectives, the ISD program proposes five analytical perspectives as the core building blocks of the programme. The programme considers that the future of enterprises—and the design of their future information systems (IS)—will be determined by the interaction between developments in socio-ethical, strategic, technological, regulatory and organisational trends. Only by considering these five perspectives, interactively and systemically, we can fully understand the reality of the driving forces affecting future companies and their information systems.

The ISD program is therefore focused on obtaining a better understanding of the relationship between the progress in the development and implementation of information systems, on the one hand, and on the their numerous impacts on organisations, industries, and society in general, on the other. Since its launch, the programme has already been supporting more than 30 projects conducted by international teams from different academic backgrounds (computer science, management science, economics, sociologists, geographers, anthropologists, etc.) as well as from different institutions, and geographical locations (Europe, North America, Asia).

The issue of digitality and digital spaces Why digital *spaces*? Several arguments convinced us that digital spaces is an important arena for research and action. The first obvious reason is that for business modelling and business action, both academics and industry practitioners fully agree that we have to transcend the traditional concept that value creation only occurs in the firm, especially when the question of the use of digital artefacts and related systems is considered. Several significant innovations have taken place outside the boundaries of the firm, as the criticality of social medias attests it. Second, digitality engenders a profound and surprisingly silent revolution in the way activities are organised and linked in different spaces, thus challenging the way we traditionally view and analytically deconstruct organisations. The generativity of digital technology is now considered a significant epistemological perspective and possibly as a substitute for the analytical one.[1] Third, and more fundamentally, there is a great potential for the use of digital spaces for value creation and extraction by firms in the market economy, due to the intrinsic nature of digitality: (1) it creates a new medium for value creation (social media, mobility etc..), as an extension of the physical/geographical media; (2) it allows the link between existing physical spaces and new spaces and (3) it allows the acceleration of links among different spaces (hence the concept of acceluction presented hereafter). These three arguments fundamentally support the view that digital spaces extend beyond collaborations within and around organisations: they represent deep transformations in not only our business ecosystems, including the way business models are designed and implemented, but more generally, our daily lives.

The Acceluction concept .... For an accelucted enterprise The importance of the behaviour of firms in this new digital space calls for a renewed aradigmatic approach to business modelling and practices. Several critical issues are posed: (i) How must firms organise for value creation in digital spaces?; (ii) Are there specific governance mechanisms that need to be considered?; (iii) How can we articulate between "internal" and "external" resources in the digital spaces?; (iv) How do we deal with intellectual property rights (IPR) issues?' (v) Are there specific local and regional practices that need to be considered?; (vi) and more generally how do we conceptually characterise the emerging space of digitality?

Based on the results of the first step of the ISD programme, I have introduced the concept of *acceluction*[2] as a way of delineating firms and societal behaviours in the

---

[1] Yoo et al. (2010). The next wave of digital innovation: opportunities and challenges. Report on the research workshop: "Digital challenges in innovation research", Temple university. Available at: http://papers.ssrn.com/sol3/papers.cfm?abstract_id=1622170

[2] Bounfour (2011). Acceluction in Action: An Overview of Wave A Projects. *International Research Programme on Information Systems Dynamics*. Paris: CIGREF Foundation (www.fondation-cigref.org)

new digital spaces. Acceluction is proposed as a new paradigm of value production in the digital spaces. According to this concept, a new type of firm is emerging—the accelucted enterprise, where the main driver for value creation lies in the accelerated production of links between different spaces, corporate, communities, society as a whole. These links might be transactional, e.g. subject to more or less spot economic transactions, or organic, e.g. a type of links governed by recognition principle, or a hybrid (e.g. both transactional and to a certain degree organic).

Business modelling in the digital spaces This book, "Business Modelling in the Dynamic Digital Space", is an important contribution to the design of the *accelucted enterprise*, especially from the 2020 perspective. Taking a mid-term time perspective, El Sawy and Pereira articulate the deep changes in the game that the 2020 enterprise will face, induced by three main drivers: the primacy of the customer experience, the distributed cocreation of value and the continuous sense-and-response experimentation. Obviously, digital systems, technology and artifacts are key components and facilitators to such a major transformation of the enterprises' ecosystems. They are at the heart of the transformation and a key component of the ecosystem. This book is a timely key contribution to the digital agenda, not only because it provides a renewed analytical and forward-looking perspective, but also because the authors took a further step by providing an overall framework for business modelling in the digital arena: VISOR, as a unified framework for business modelling in the digital space. The framework is articulated around five components for business modelling: Value proposition, Interface, Service Platforms, Organising model and Revenue Model. Some of the items are also suggested by other frameworks, but VISOR presents the advantage of being fully dedicated to the digital spaces and particularly incorporates a service platform dimension. The proposed model is then applied in detail on three case studies: NikE+, Humana and Zipcar, attesting to its potential of deployment and feasibility. Using a scenario construction approach, the final chapter extends the analyses of these firms, and their performance in their respective industries in 2020. Through its sequences, this book provides two stimulating extension to the analysis in business modelling: first by introducing other actors of value creation (clients, complementors...) to the traditional firm spaces and second, by developing several plausible future scenarios. The whole model is well balanced theoretically, and also appealing for its practical dimension. I am sure that both scholars and business decision makers—including CIOs—will find reading this book helpful not only in their daily work, but also in their mid- and long-term strategic thinking. This book is a welcome and timely overview of business modelling, with a practical orientation and I am very delighted that this book inaugurates the SpringerBriefs Series on Digital Spaces.

Ahmed Bounfour
Professor, University Paris-Sud
European Chair on Intellectual capital management
Rapporteur General, ISD programme
Editor, *SpringerBriefs in Digital Spaces*

Contents

Executive Summary

This research study[1] seeks to examine how through systematic modeling and better conceptualization, we can help enterprises to better navigate through the digital business model world of 2020, and design more effective digital business models for the enterprise, the business ecosystem, and society. It seeks to answer what will be the likely critical game changers for the enterprise in the year 2020 in a digitally intensive world, and how that will influence the types of digital business models that successful enterprises will want to adopt. Our aim is to help design more effective digital business models for the enterprise, the business ecosystem, and society.

A. Research Objectives
Specifically, this study was designed to achieve the following:

- Development of a systematic unified modeling framework for digital business models, and articulating its components in an operationalized fashion.
- Understanding the dynamics of the digital business ecosystem and its critical game changers with an eye toward the enterprise in the year 2020.
- Illustration of the framework and method through enterprise case examples.
- Derivation of forward looking views and scenarios for novel digital business models for enterprises in 2020.

B. Modalities of Conduct
To achieve the above stated objectives, the following methods of investigation were used :

- Extensive review and analysis of past work in research and practice on digital business models and ecological views of strategy in the areas of strategic management, organizations, and information systems.

[1] We would like to thank Foundation CIGREF for a generous grant which help support this work. We also would like to thank and acknowledge Joseph W. Clark, Ph.D. Candidate at the Marshall School of Business for all his contributions and insights in this project.

- Drawing on the research findings and the industry experiences of the Institute of Communication Technologies Management (CTM) at the Marshall School of Business, University of Southern California which is an industry-facing center that focuses on the telecom, content, entertainment, and media industries.
- Case studies drawn from public sources of information, with some supporting interviews from managers in case study companies.
- Scenario generation and what-if analysis for digital business models for enterprises in 2020.

C. Description of the Report

The report is divided into five chapters:

Chapter 1 articulates the dynamics of digital business ecosystems and identifies some key game changers for the enterprise in 2020 to help provide the context in which new digital business models will be designed, implemented, assessed, and changed. It shows that value is created, converted, and captured beyond the enterprise, and in concert with customers, competitors, complementors, and community. It also examines core shifts in digital platforms and societal trends while identifying three core game changers for the enterprise in the year 2020: the primacy of the customer experience, distributed co-creation of value, and continuous sense-and-respond experimentation.

Chapter 2 examines the origins and history of business models in general, and digital business models in particular through a review and analysis of past work. It shows some of the disparities and lack of synthesis across business model frameworks, little theory-based conceptualization, and often no specific consideration of the special features that services offered through digital platforms bring to business models such as user experience and interface factors.

Chapter 3 proposes a "unified framework" for business models that resolve those issues through a unified modeling framework that provides a systematic common language. We have termed it the VISOR framework and it has five key components: value proposition, interface, service platform, organizing model, and revenue model. We articulate each of those components with operationalized descriptors, and show how the framework can be used in the context of the evolving digital business ecosystem and the game changers it brings with it.

Chapter 4 examines three case studies of digital business models through the VISOR framework. We pick three companies that are in relatively mature industries (athletic shoes, car rental, and healthcare) and show how they changed their business models by taking advantage of digital platforms in an evolving environment. The VISOR framework helps to systematically examine and assess the many facets of those digital models allowing better analysis and an articulated unified framework that managers from different functional areas can discuss with a common language whether they are from marketing, operations, technology, or finance.

Chapter 5 applies the VISOR palette in a creative and mind-stretching mode by looking forward to 2020 and deriving scenarios for enterprises in the same industries whose example case we analyzed in Chap. 4. We use each of the three game core changers that we identified in Chap. 1, and we "yank" each of them to an extreme position to be able to imagine new digital business models under those conditions. We then pivot around the various VISOR components to operationalize new business models. This yanking exercise helps to derive new business model designs that would not otherwise be apparent to academic facilitators or managers, and shows how current models could be redesigned.

Implications of this Study

This report has implications for academicians, managers, and society in general.

(a) **At the Scientific Level**

- The development of the VISOR conceptual framework as a unified framework for digital business models.
- Articulating operational descriptors for each of the components of the VISOR framework.
- Espousing an ecological view of strategy and expositing how value is created, converted, and captured beyond the enterprise, and in concert with customers, competitors, complementors, and community.
- Using scenario generation methods to derive novel digital business models.

(b) **At the Managerial Level**

- Identifying likely game changers in the digital business ecosystem for the enterprise in 2020.
- Providing VISOR framework as a tool for managers from different functional areas to help design and assess novel digital business models.
- Providing case study examples that illustrate how the VISOR framework can serve as a guide for understanding and improvement.
- Devising a scenario generation method that uses extreme "yanking" on critical game changers in concert with the VISOR framework that results in novel digital business models.

(c) **At the Societal Level**

- A realization that the ecosystem view of digital business ecosystems goes beyond the enterprise and involves co-creation with customers and community, which ties the managerial level with the societal level in a much more interdependent way than in the past.
- The derivation of critical game changers for the enterprise in 2020 are based on interactions with shifts in digital platforms and shifts in societal value, and together they holistically constitute the dynamics of digital business ecosystems. Thus increasingly in the future, societal values will play an increasingly intrinsic role in the design and deployment of digital business models.

D. Contribution to the Objective/Key Topics of Information System Dynamic (ISD) Programs

We believe this study helps achieve the objectives of the ISD Program in the following manner:

- This study is located at the intersection of IT/IS, and the strategic management of organizations, business ecosystems, and societies. It contributes to the area of business models in the digital space which is one of the areas that is key in building a future where IT/IS plays an increasing important role.
- The study is forward looking with an eye toward the enterprise in the year 2020 and how to design novel digital business models for that future using extreme scenarios. This is in line with the forward looking approach of the ISD Program.
- The study embraces an ecosystem perspective that like the ISD Program goes beyond the enterprise and embraces the larger domain of society and community.
- The study helps to provide an analytical and systematic approach that can be used by managers for better understanding of the design and assessment of digital business models.

Chapter 1
Anticipating Game Changers for "Enterprise 2020" in a Digitally-Intensive World

What will be the critical game changers for the enterprise in the year 2020 in a digitally-intensive world? How will that influence the types of digital business models that successful enterprises will want to adopt? And how can we through systematic modeling and better conceptualization help enterprises better navigate through the digital business model world of 2020, and design more effective digital business models for the enterprise, the business ecosystem, and society?

This opening orientation chapter seeks to articulate the dynamics of digital business ecosystems and identify some key game changers for the enterprise in 2020 to help provide the context in which new digital business models will be designed, implemented, assessed, and changed.

The chapter adopts a dynamic and holistic view of the digital business ecosystem and its evolution through the simultaneous shifts in technology, societal trends, and enterprise practices. The chapter identifies key shifts that are already emerging in technology and societal trends with an eye towards 2020. We then focus on key game changes for the enterprise in the year 2020 related to value creation, value conversion, and value capture in digital business ecosystems.

1.1 The Dynamics of the Digital Business Ecosystem

As the world becomes more digitally-intensive and the business environment becomes more turbulent, the boundaries between digital platforms, enterprises, and environments are becoming more blurred. The simultaneous increase in environmental turbulence and societal change, the requisite speed of organizational change, and the intensified ubiquity of digital technologies are spawning a digital business ecosystem that is constantly evolving and unfolding dynamically. Increasingly enterprises find themselves in the midst of that digital business

O. A. El Sawy and F. Pereira, *Business Modelling in the Dynamic Digital Space*,
SpringerBriefs in Digital Spaces, DOI: 10.1007/978-3-642-31765-1_1,
© The Author(s) 2013

ecosystem in which products and services are increasingly provided through digital platforms.

Digital business ecosystems evolve at an ever-accelerating pace, driven by intense competition and rapidly-improving technological capabilities (El Sawy et al. 1999). The velocity of exchange in digital business ecosystems has a number of implications. First, it means that competitive advantage is short-lived. Strategies are perishable, whether attained by first-mover advantage, advantageous positioning vis-à-vis the marketplace, or unique capabilities. Thus, even within the resource-based view, it turns out that the most important capabilities are not the ones that deliver products and services, but the dynamic capabilities that modify those primary capabilities, such as R&D, marketing, new product development, and business process re-engineering (Eisenhardt and Martin 2000; Winter 2003) and improvisational capabilities (Pavlou and El Sawy 2010) that enable firms to cope with unexpected changes. In this context, we see agility, rather than advantageous positioning, as the key to meeting strategic opportunities and threats (Teece 2007; Sambamurthy et al. 2003; Overby et al. 2006). Technologies and services rapidly become obsolete in the digital business ecosystem. Therefore, constant innovation is not just an advantage: it is a necessity to even play the game.

Digital business ecosystems are not only fast-paced, they are also turbulent. Turbulence is a causal texture of the environment that stems from complex interconnectedness between players (Selsky et al. 2007). In turbulent environments, changes to strategic variables are not only rapid but also unexpected, as disruptions may come at any time from firms innovating in different fields (Burgelman and Grove 2007) or from the larger society. Unlike other business environments, digital business ecosystems can never be expected to revert to any kind of "equilibrium" after disruptions change things; turbulence implies that cause-and-effect may cascade in unpredictable ways to alter the structure or health of the ecosystem, or end it entirely. Preparing for these "unknown unknowns" requires a new kind of management sensibility: an ability to develop new frameworks and perspectives, and a strategic eye for vulnerability to "black swan" events (Meyer et al. 2005; Taleb 2007). Because the fates of all players are intertwined with that of the ecosystem, competitors must often work together in "coopetition", for example to establish technical standards or common platforms. Through constant interaction, business models and digital innovations coevolve, and we cannot truly understand their trajectories if we examine each one in isolation (Boland et al. 2007).

The manifestations of the dynamic of digital business ecosystems are all around us at both the organizational and industry level. Burgelman and Grove (2007) have shown how industry boundaries are systemically disrupted through novel digital platforms, dynamic capabilities, and opportunities in the environment. For example, through its digital devices and technology platforms, Apple has disrupted the dynamics of the business environment and influenced the development of dynamic capabilities in the music (iPod), smartphone (iPhone), software (App store), and publishing (iPad) industries. But it required dynamic capabilities that

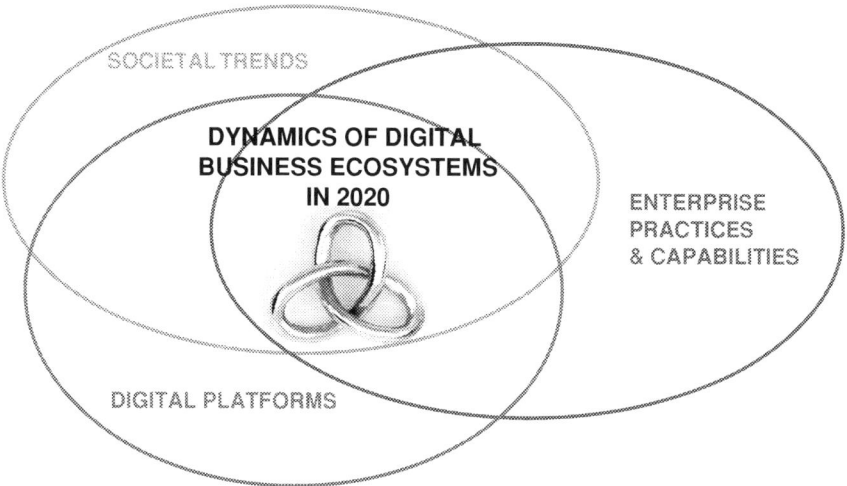

Fig. 1.1 A holistic view of the dynamics of digital business ecosystems

enabled them to be first movers and alliance brokers in a market environment that was ready for their new product introductions. Similarly, the advent of Web 2.0 technologies (c.f., Wagner and Majchrzak 2007) has altered the nature of inter-active collaboration and intellectual capabilities, thus spawning environmental turbulence in the realms of product design, marketing, and R&D—but that was accompanied by a mindset of open innovation and global open sourcing. These examples highlight the novel and complex characteristics exhibited by the dynamics of digital business ecosystems.

Given the fused dynamic interactions between the many elements of the digital business ecosystem, it is appropriate to view its unfolding dynamics as a systemic and holistic phenomenon that capture its complexity. Figure 1.1 graphically illustrates a holistic view of the interactions among three key elements of the digital business ecosystem that are of interest to our study: digital platform, societal trends, and enterprise practices and capabilities. The interactions are represented through the intersecting orbits in the figure, but it also signals the fusion quality of digital business ecosystems through an entangled Gordian knot at the center. The digital business ecosystem has no separations among those three core elements, but it is the wholeness of the fused interactions among the three elements.

This depiction captures the fusion of IT systems with the dynamics of orga-nizations and the unrest of the environment in a way that is well-suited to a world of increased digital intensity in industry after industry: financial services, retail, travel, entertainment, healthcare, energy,…, thus transforming the way that organizations function, compete, thrive, and innovate. *Business Week's* 2010 list of the Top 50 innovative organizations shows over half of them to be in the digital space and part of the growing supply side of the growing digital ecosystem. The digital revolution that became most apparent with the Internet boom-bust in the late-1990s is finally taking hold in a transformational way across a large number of organizations and industries. When IT becomes part of the fabric of organizations and entire industries, the perspective of digital business ecosystems becomes an organizing vision.

1.2 Value Creation, Value Conversion, and Value Capture in Digital Business Ecosystems

A digital business ecosystems approach brings with it a number of changes in how value is created, how value is converted, and how value is captured (cf. Lepak et al. 2007). First, the whole notion of value changes in a digitally intensive world. Second, value is co-created, co-converted, and co-captured together with the different players in the ecosystem: customers, competitors, complementors, and community—and it becomes a much more complex process. Third, it is necessary to take into account the rapid shift in trends in digital platforms, societal values, and enterprise practices and capabilities as they co-evolve.

Many schools of thought in economics and management treat value as "utility" embedded in goods and services, or "value-in-exchange" measurable by the prices consumers are willing to pay. From this perspective, the role of the enterprise is to *add* value to raw materials, or *deliver* value to customers. We diagram businesses as "value chains" of value-adding activities, or as any of a variety of different forms such as "value shops" and "value networks" (Stabell and Fjeldstad 1998). Theories of strategic management argue that firm strengths result in competitive advantage if they add more value ("effectiveness"), or deliver value at lower costs ("efficiency") than competitors (Barney 1991). This view of value has been with us since the time of Adam Smith, whose economic analysis focused on the commodity exports of goods-producing nations, and has yielded many insights. However, when we move away from the basic model of goods manufacturers making standardized products, we find that this conceptualization of value no longer fits. Value-in-exchange is a useful tool for talking about coal, steel, or wheat, but we have to jump through theoretical hoops to describe the value-in-exchange of a digital service, or of a concept like "mobility" (Lee et al. 2010).

In digital business ecosystems, products and services are complex, customized, and made up of modular components provided by networks of firms. In the case of digital products like mobile phones, for example, customers using the same hardware will rarely if ever make all of the same software choices, or use the devices in the same ways and in the same contexts. Customers' willingness to pay, too, will vary greatly. Instead of assuming value is delivered in standard quantities by digital products and services, then, it is more useful to see value as an experience created through use and perceived by each customer upon the enactment of a digital service. This perspective of "value-in-use" or "value-as-experience" or "value conversion" is embodied in Theodore Levitt's famous example of the drill: "customers do not want a drill; they want the holes that the drill will make" (cf. Chesbrough 2011). This is even more true in digital business ecosystems. Digital services, unlike drills, do not even come off an assembly line looking the same.

The value conversion perspective was written about by strategy researchers Normann and Ramírez (1993) and in recent years has grown into a bold new logic of value creation in the marketing field (Vargo and Lusch 2004, 2008) called the service-dominant logic (SDL), this new theory holds that value is co-created by customers and a network of firms and other actors. Whether these actors are providing activities (services), or "frozen activities" in the forms of products (like Levitt's drill), what they are really exchanging are applications of capabilities, skills, and knowledge. Thus products and services are best thought of as value *offerings* or *propositions*. They have *potential* value that may or may not be exercised by customers. To create value, then, firms and customers are partners. Firms develop and deliver potentially-valuable offerings, and customers assemble and utilize these offerings in context to realize value. Value is phenomenologically experienced and contextually interpreted by the customer (Vargo and Lusch 2008; Chesbrough 2011). Thus value conversion is a subsequent step after value creation.

This paradigm draws our attention to the importance of the unique characteristics of customers and the contexts in which they use services. One of the key takeaways from the service-dominant logic is that *no service occurs unless customers apply the offering* (activity or product) in context. We may be used to thinking of a firm's services as activities that it *can* provide. That may be appropriate when a firm's service offerings are standardized and repeated—it's analogous to treating services as commodity products—but when studying digital business ecosystems where every enactment of a service is unique, we must study value creation by focusing on how service offerings are (and are not) actually applied. This leaves us with no good answer to the question of how managers can appropriate, or even measure, the value that they are co-creating with customers through digital services.

The literature of strategic management, by contrast, has a long tradition of theorizing about value appropriation in competition. The dominant strategy paradigm at the firm level of analysis is the *resource-based view* (RBV) in which competitive advantage accrues to firms that have control of strategically important resources, such as assets and capabilities (Barney 1991). In its basic form, the RBV states that resources must be valuable (have value-creating *potential*), rare among competitors, imperfectly imitable, and non-substitutable—the so-called "VRIN" characteristics—in order to be sources of competitive advantage. Combining the RBV with the value creation logic just discussed, one might argue that if a firm has a VRIN capability to perform an activity better, faster, or cheaper (from the customer's point of view) than its competitors, its value proposition is more likely to be accepted.

The VRIN conditions do not always hold, and are especially problematic in digital business ecosystems where capabilities evolve and become obsolete quickly, technologies are often substitutable for one another, and service-oriented, pay-for-use business models mean that powerful competencies are equally accessible to the largest and smallest competitors. These empirical problems have led some researchers to develop new variations on RBV theory to explain value appropriation in less ideal environments. The first variation argues that firms can profit from services in which they have no VRIN advantages as long as they have complementary assets that are VRIN (Teece 1986). This explains why IBM, which has VRIN capabilities in hardware and applications, would be willing to embrace the non-proprietary operating system Linux (West 2003). While IBM captures no value from sales of Linux, the widespread adoption of Linux allows it to capture value from its complementary offerings.

The *relational view* (RV) is a variation on the RBV in which individual firms may have no VRIN resources at all, but may yet attain competitive advantages if they form alliances that have VRIN *combinations* of resources (Dyer and Singh 1998). A related concept is that of *cospecialization* of resources; resources may be designed such that they have greater value potential together than separately (Teece 1986). We might suppose, for example, that Intel's microprocessors and Microsoft's operating systems are not VRIN by themselves, but being designed to work in concert, the combination of the two may have unique advantages compared to other platforms. An interesting question is whether the RV theory applies the same way to *platforms* as it does to alliances. In the years since Dyer and Singh (1998) wrote about dyadic alliances possessing VRIN resource com-binations, we have seen a rise in the importance of digital platforms (Gawer and Cusumano 2008; Iansiti and Levien 2004). Defined by standard architectures and interfaces, platforms allow modular connection of activities and resources across firms. Platforms are less exclusive than alliances, but potentially much more powerful. The *open resource-based view* (Schlagwein et al. 2010) extends the relational view from formal alliances to open platforms, and also uses comple-mentarity and cospecialization or resources to explain value creation, conversion, and capture.

Thus, in a digital business ecosystem, value is co-created, co-converted, and co-captured together with the different players in the ecosystem: customers, competitors, complementors, and community (see Fig. 1.2). In such a digital business ecosystem, one of the key issues is the balance between value creation, value conversion, and value capture (Iansiti and Levien 2004). Thus, enterprises in keystone positions in the ecosystem may choose to leave many activities of value creation to others in the ecosystem, while choosing to focus on creating value that is critical to the ecosystem's prosperity. In digital business ecosystems, this may mean the creation of common digital platforms for the delivery of digital services whose value can be shared with the entire ecosystem, such that value conversion can take place. However, it also needs to ensure that it can capture part of the value. This balancing act between different players in a business ecosystem becomes much more complex when we are dealing with a digital business ecosystem. It also means the design of effective digital business models for the

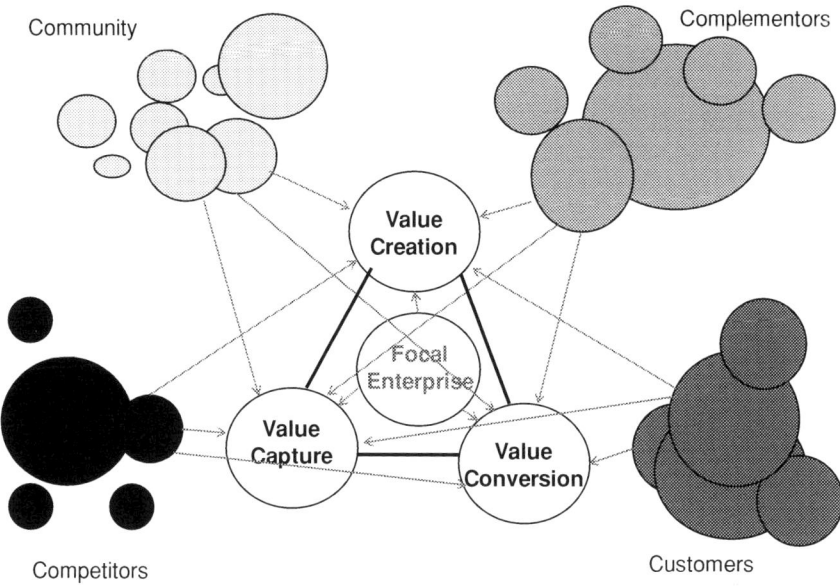

Community   Complementors

Value
Creation

Focal
Enterprise

Value
Capture   Value
                                Conversion

Competitors   Customers

** Size of circle represents influence in ecosystem

Fig. 1.2 Value map of digital business ecosystem

enterprise in such ecosystem conditions becomes more critical for survival and thriving. This requires an awareness of core changes and shifts in the ecosystem.

1.3 Depicting Core Shifts in the Digital Business Ecosystem

We have identified core shifts in the ecosystem around the three critical areas that we believe are key to designing more effective digital business models in 2020: digital platforms, societal trends, and how value is co-created in the enterprise. They form a holistic interactive whole and influence each other. This is depicted in Fig. 1.3.

The emerging evolutions and disruptions in digital platforms that are taking hold are the easiest to identify. While technological change is rapid, the adoption of new digital platforms in mass scale such that it influences the deep structure of the ecosystem takes a longer time (El Sawy et al. 2010). For many years, the analyst firm Gartner has studied the technology adoption hype cycle and has shown that typically after an initial hype phase, all technological changes go through a period of diminished expectations, then the ones that survive and are adopted in mass scale go through a period of enlightenment where effective solutions and actionable innovations can be achieved by enterprises.

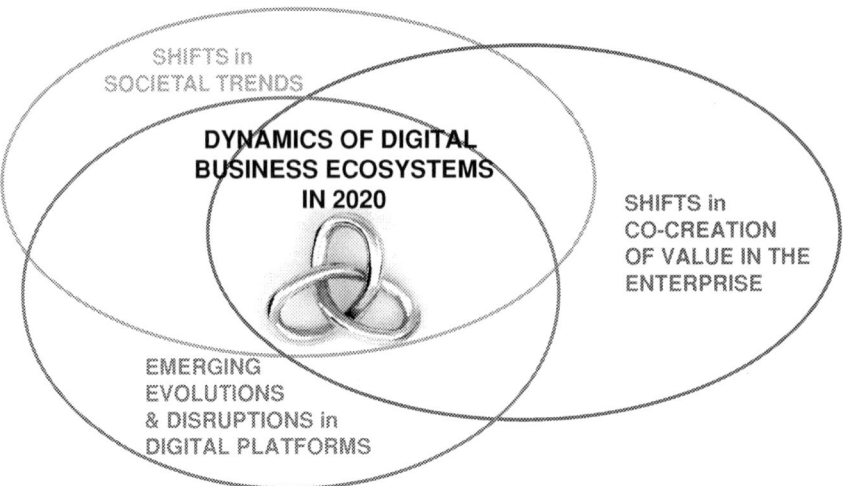

Fig. 1.3 Depicting core changes in digital business ecosystems

Table 1.1 Key changes in digital platforms with an eye towards 2020

Key changes in digital platforms	Explanation	Likely impact
The rapid growth of the "Internet of things"	The forceast is for billions of sensors and devices to be connected to the internet, and growth of machine-to-machine communication	This will generate a flood of data on the internet, as well as further bring to prominence the need for data analytics
The proliferation of broadband cloud computing	Computer hardware, software, and data will be hosted on the cloud	Enterprises will have have the digital capabilities to be highly flexible and scale quickly
The spread of service-oriented architecture and modular applications	Software applications will be aggregated through lego-like smaller components	Enterprises will be able to put together new application software "on the fly"
The proliferation of untethered smartphones with multisensory interaction	Smartphone devices will take advantage of haptics, body computing, and avanced voice recognition	The ubiquity and richness of interaction with digital devices and interfaces, will be unprecedented
Augmented reality becomes practically useful	Our real-world environment will be enhanced through computer-generaated sensory input	We will finally be able to integrated digital technologies into our physical world much more effectively

Table 1.2 Key changes in societal values with an eye towards 2020

Key changes in societal values	Explanation	Likely impact
Sustainability becomes a dominant value	An emphasis on conservation of resources, and not compromising future generations	Strategy for sustainability as a business opportunity, rather than a constraint will yield new business models for the bottom of the pyramid
Transparency is an expected norm	Making actions, processes, and relationships visible	Progressive companies will use digital technologies to augment transparency
Open source sharing and peering	A volunteerism and sharing of efforts and opinions with peers	Social media will become the dominant mode of interaction and relationships
Digital attention disorder	The ubiquity of continuous internet access and multitasking leads to continuous partial attention	Attention will be very scarce resource, and services based on business models that conserve it will be highly valued
The rise of glocalization	The combination of a global outlook and the need to preserve the local culture and context	A new form of global markets will emerge that are both connected and segmented

Our survey of the technological landscape for such changes in digital platforms through our knowledge of the industry through repeated interaction with CTM participating companies suggests that a number of such changes. We have identified five of those as being most likely to influence the structure of the digital business ecosystem in the year 2020. They are shown in Table 1.1 with an explanation of why they are likely to be influential shifts.

Similarly, we have identified a number of shifts in societal values worldwide. We have identified five of those as being most likely to influence the structure of the digital business ecosystem in the year 2020. They are shown in Table 1.2 with an explanation of why they are likely to be influential shifts.

These key changes in digital platforms and societal values interact with each other and the way that value is created in enterprises. We examine in the next section how the impacts of the changes that we have identified above will influence the enterprise in 2020. We articulate those changes for the enterprise in the form of what we have called game changers.

1.4 Game Changers for Enterprise 2020

There are many definitions of game changers, and many contexts for game changers. A person who is a visionary is often referred to as a game changer. An enterprise which conceives a new strategy in its industry or ecosystem—and that forces or induces other players to fundamentally change their strategies—is often

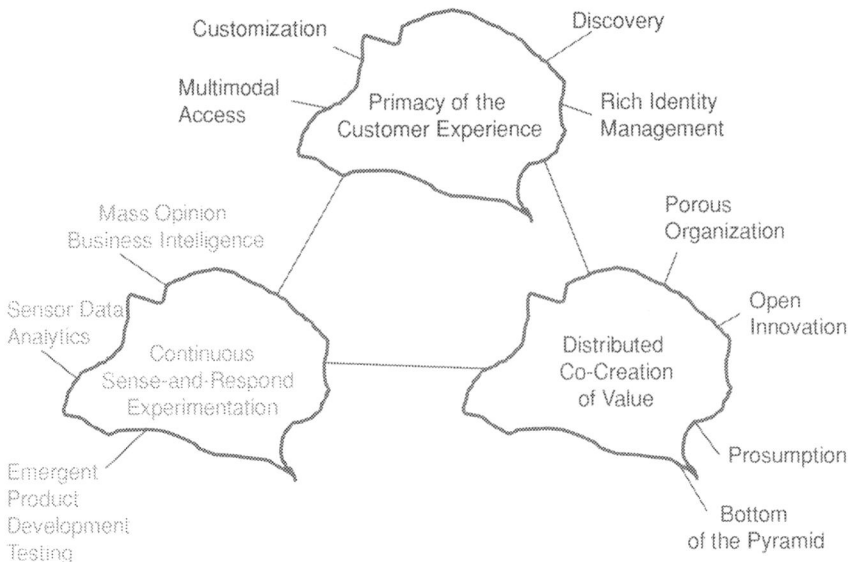

Fig. 1.4 Key games changers for enterprise 2020 related to value creation, conversion, and capture

referred to as a game changer. An idea or an event that completely changes the way a situation develops is referred to as a game changer. Radically changing the way that something is done or thought about is referred to as a game changer. A disruptive event or crisis that disrupts industry boundaries or changes the rules of competition, or changes the fabric of a social order or society is often referred to as a game changer. Similarly, evolutionary changes which gather critical mass and momentum and are adopted by a large number of people can be game changers. So, for example the adoption of social networks (such as FaceBook) has been a game changer in how social relationships are maintained, how people interact and communicate, and how they share ideas. And that game changer in turn (in the case of social networks for example) can also trigger and enable other phenomena which in turn also become game changers at the next level such as crowdsourcing, or open innovation, or management by consensus. Thus, game changers can also occur or be created in a cascaded manner over time. Thus, technological shifts and societal value shifts can beget enterprise game changers. Drawing on those two sets of shifts and their implications, we then show how they cascade into a set of enterprise phenomena that are likely to be game changers for the enterprise of 2020.

We have combined the implications of Tables 1.1 and 1.2 and come up with three key game changers for the enterprise in 2020 related to value creation, value conversion, and value capture. They are: the primacy of the customer experience, distributed co-creation of value, and continuous sense-and-respond experimentation. They are depicted in Fig. 1.4 in addition to the phenomena that accompany them, thus creating a constellation around the game changer. They are further explained below:

1.4.1 Game Changer #1 for Enterprise 2020: Primacy of the Customer Experience

As pointed out in Sect. 1.2, in a world of experiential goods and digital services, the customer experience becomes primate as value is primarily created through the process of consumption and the experience which it creates. Designing more effective customer experiences around services provided through digital platforms will take center stage in designing new digital business models. With the shifts in digital platforms and societal values outlined above, there will be a constellation of phenomena around this game changer. First, the notion of customization and personalization will become very elaborate and sophisticated. Second, each consumer will own a digital rich identity on the internet that captures his or her preferences, tastes, interests, etc. and this with further enable customization and targeting. Third, given the scarcity of attention and the need for personalization, the dominant paradigm on the internet will change from search to discovery, in which services learn a customer's preferences and discover them, sometimes proactively. Fourth, this primacy of experience will be further augmented by multiple modes of access and devices with multisensory capabilities. This game changing constellation will transform the digital business models of enterprises in 2020.

1.4.2 Game Changer #2 for Enterprise 2020: Distributed Co-Creation of Value

As pointed out in Sect. 1.2, the way that value is created, converted, and captured is complex and different in digital business ecosystems. With the shifts in digital platforms and societal values outlined above, this will become a game changer for enterprises in 2020, especially in terms of the different ways that value is co-created with customers, competitors, complementors and community. The trends suggest that there will be a constellation of phenomena around this game changer. First, with distributed co-creation of value the boundaries of the enterprise will be much more porous and it will be more difficult to define where the enterprise ends and the other parts of the ecosystem begin. Second, open innovation will likely be a dominant mode of operations as new products and services need to come to market more quickly for diverse customers. Third, the notion of prosumption will take hold as consumers of services and products engage in their production through processes that we are already seeing in phenomena such as user-generated content. Fourth, with the emphasis on sustainability and glocal-ization, we will see much more emphasis on the poor of the world or as they are often called "the bottom of the pyramid." This game changing constellation will transform the digital business models of enterprises in 2020.

1.4.3 Game Changer #3 for Enterprise 2020: Continuous Sense-and-Respond Experimentation

The key changes in digital platforms with the proliferation of ubiquitous access, ease of capturing data, and digital services, will enable enterprises to engage in continuous sense-and-respond experimentation in ways they could not before. The launch of new products and services will be accompanied by digital online pilots that can cheaply and easily gather information. The trends suggest that there will be a constellation of phenomena around this game changer. First, most new and emergent product testing will be done through online experiments in which products are tweaked and emerge continuously over time. Second, with all the burgeoning of sensor data, there will be a surge in sophistication in sensor data analytics that will enable intelligent interpretation of data. Third, business intel-ligence will become rooted around social media and networks, and we will be able to troll social media for market insights. The whole area of mass opinion business intelligence combined with sensor data analytics will give enterprises tremendous new capabilities for sense-and-respond experimentation. This game changing constellation will transform the digital business models of enterprises in 2020.

These three game changers provide the context for the enterprise in 2020 in which new digital business models will be designed and assessed, and we use them to generate scenarios and configurations for digital business models for Enterprise 2020 in Chap. 5 of this document.

Chapter 2
Digital Business Models: Review and Synthesis

2.1 Origins of Business Models

While technological disruptions are changing the competitive landscape, their full impact on business structures, processes, and innovativeness are less understood and vary significantly across companies in the same industry, and may ironically be similar for companies in different industries. A primary reason for such a seemingly "random process" is the lack of a generally accepted definition of the term "business model" within which to provide systematic analyses. In fact, multiple definitions of business models exist, which pose significant challenges for understanding essential components.

In general, there is no accepted definition of the term "business model" (Shafer et al. 2005; Ho et al. 2010; Muller et al. 2011). Although, the origins of the expression business model can be traced back to the writings of Peter Drucker (Ramon et al. 2009), the concept had gained prominence only in the last decade or two. Many have observed that the term "business model" became widely adopted by practitioners during the dotcom revolution of the 1990s. While business model has been part of the business jargon for a long time, it has been argued that the focus initially involved a scientific analysis of firms has been on industry, and resources, as shown by the works of Porter (1980) and Wernerfeld (Hoyer et al. 2009). Others, in fact, some have argued that the concept of a business model, is relatively new, dating back to only the early 1980s. Furthermore, there is little theoretical underpinning in the literature, (Linder and Cantrell 2000; Morris et al. 2006; Kalantari 2010) particularly in economic theory (Teese 2010).

The plethora of definitions poses significant challenges for understanding the essential components of a business model. They also lead to confusion in terminology as "business model, strategy, business concept, revenue model and economic model are often used interchangeably… (and moreover) the business model has been referred to as architecture, design, pattern, plan, method, assumption and statement" (Morris et al. 2005).

O. A. El Sawy and F. Pereira, *Business Modelling in the Dynamic Digital Space*, SpringerBriefs in Digital Spaces, DOI: 10.1007/978-3-642-31765-1_2, © The Author(s) 2013

For example some definitions of business models:

a. Baden-Fuller et al. when they define *business models* "the logic of the firm, the way it operates and how it creates value for its stakeholders (2000).
b. Timmers defines the business model as architecture for product, service and information flows, including a description of the various business actors and their roles; and a description of the potential benefits for various business actors; and a description of the sources of revenue (Timmers 2000).
c. Mahadevan defines a business as is a unique blend of three streams that are critical to the business. These include the value stream for the business partners and the buyers, the revenue stream and the logistical stream (Mahendran 2000).
d. Johnson et al. define "Business model consists of four interlocking elements that, taken together create and deliver value... customer value proposition... profit formula... key resources... key processes".
e. Ostenwalder et al. define "A business model is a conceptual tool containing a set of objects, concepts and their relationships with the objective to express the business logic of a specific firm. Therefore we must consider which concepts and relationships allow a simplified description and representation of what value is provided to customers, how this is done and with which financial consequences (Ostenwalder et al. 2010).
f. Teese, defines, "business articulates the logic and provides data, and other evidence that demonstrates how a business creates and delivers value to customers. It also outlines the architecture of revenues, costs, profits associated with the business enterprise delivering value" (Teese 2010).
g. Demil and Lecocq, define "business model as, the description of the articulation between different business model components or building blocks to produce a proposition that can generate value for consumers and thus for the organization" (Demil and Lecocq 2010).
h. Sorescu et al. define "a business model is a well-specified system of interdependent structures, activities, and processes that serves as a firm's organizing logic for value creation (for its customers) and value appropriation (for itself and its partners)" (Sorescu et al. 2011).

In addition, the concept of business models can be seen as having progressed in 5 stages as shown in Fig. 2.1 (Gordijn et al. 2005). In the initial phase, when the term business model started to become prominent, a number of authors suggested business model definitions and classifications. Then, during the second phase authors started to complete the definitions by proposing what elements belong into a business models. Initially, these propositions were simple shopping lists, just mentioning the components of a business model. Only in a third phase followed detailed descriptions of these components (Hamel 2000; Weill and Vitale 2001; Afuah and Tucci 2003). In a fourth phase researchers started to model the components conceptually culminating in business model ontologies. In this phase models also started to be more rigorously evaluated or tested. Finally, in the fifth phase, the reference models are being applied in management and IS applications.

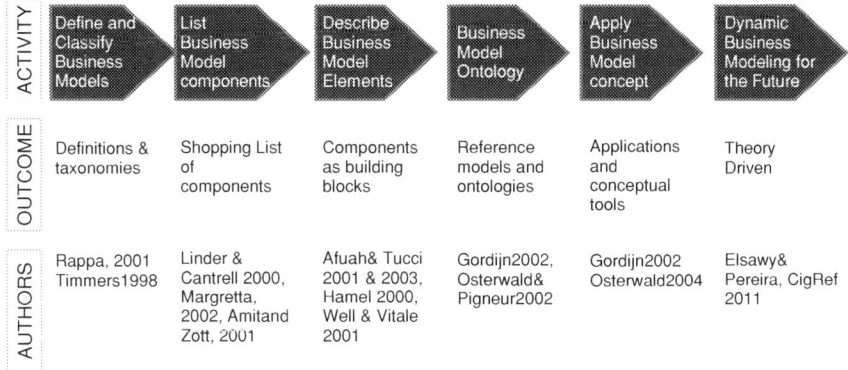

Fig. 2.1 Progression of business model studies

We assert that in the sixth phase, the focus is now on theory building and dynamic modeling.

A business model is a representation of the strategic choices that characterize a business venture. These choices are made either intentionally or by default, so the contribution of a business model is to make them explicit (Morris et al. 2005). Thus, the business model can be seen as a communication or a planning tool. It allows entrepreneurs, investors, and partners to examine strategic choices for internal consistency, to surface the assumptions of the business plan, and to understand the vision toward which the business is being built. Business model development may be part of new venture planning, but is often just as useful in sense making around a going concern, or when new opportunities and threats indicate a need for reinvention (Johnson et al. HBR 2008).

Furthermore, although properly formed business models are very useful and can be a strategic tool for a firm, many business models however suffer from 4 common problems (Shafer et al. 2005), namely:

- Flawed or untested assumptions underlying the key premises of a firm's business plan; these resolve around untested assumptions about future conditions, or implicit or explicit cause-and effect-relationships that are not well founded or logical.
- Limitations in the strategic choices considered; addressing and developing the business logic in only one "component" of the business model, and making untested assumptions about the others.
- Misunderstanding about value creation and value capture; the inability of organizations to financially capitalize on the "value" they create, which may thus negatively affect the "revenue generation" aspects of business models.
- Flawed assumptions about the value network; assumptions that the current value created through the network would continue unchanged into the future and not change dynamically.

Table 2.1 summarizes some of the attempts to capture the concept of business models over the last two decades or so. The number of components proposed in each model ranges from 3 to 9. In general, three general categories of definitions based on their emphasis, namely economic, operational and strategic, each with their unique set of decision variables have been identified (Morris et al. 2005). The economic approach focuses on how a firm can make a profit and key variables from this approach include revenue sources, pricing methodologies, cost structures, margins and expected volumes. Fundamentally stated, this approach deals with how a firm can make money and sustain its revenue stream into the future (Stewart et al. 2000). Alternatively, the operational approach focuses on the firm's internal processes and design of infrastructure that enables firms to create value, with key components such as production or service delivery methods, administrative processes, resource flow and knowledge management, with the objective of key designing interdependent systems that create and sustain a competitive business (Mayo and Brown 1999). In the strategic approach, emphasis in on the overall direction of the firm's marketing position, interactions across organizational boundaries, and growth opportunities. This approach espouses the totality of how a firm selects its customers, defines and differentiates its offerings, creates utility for its customers, define the tasks it will perform or outsource, configures its resources and ultimately captures profits (Slywotzky 1996). Decision variables focus on stakeholder identification, value creation, visions, values and networks and alliances.

2.2 Why Digital Business Models

The role of information technology and its relationship to the business has shifted over the last 20 years. We have progressively transitioned from a focus on the design of information systems, to the design of IT-enabled business processes, and more recently to the design of business models for services provided through digital platforms (Fig. 2.2). While this attention to business models for digital platforms initially started in the networked digital industry (telecom, media, entertainment, gaming. software, etc.) it is increasingly being propagated to all industries whether healthcare, energy, retail, or financial services. As more customers consume products and services offered through digital platforms, the managerial stakes in understanding those models is becoming much higher, especially when these products and services have to be offered to and priced for consumers. A review of Table 2.1 also illustrates that most of the espoused business models do not consider explicitly the effects of digital platforms specifically.

Thus, digital business ecosystems are new and different. Companies operate in a technology-enabled and digitally interconnected environment characterized by new affordances, structures, and rules (El Sawy et al. 1999). The information systems discipline has explored and explicated many of these differences. One of its most important conclusions is that technology and business are effectively fused

Table 2.1 Comparison of business model approaches

Source	Components	Number of components	Eco-system	Digital platform
Horowitz (1996)	Price, product, distribution, organizational characteristics and technology	5	No	Some
Viscio and Pasternak (1996)	Global core, governance, business units, services and linkages	5	No	No
Timmers (1998)	Product/service/information flow architecture, business actors and roles, actor benefits, revenue sources, and marketing strategy	5	No	Some
Markides (1999)	Product innovation, customer relationship, infrastructure management, and financial aspects	4	No	No
Donath (1999)	Customer understanding, marketing tactics, corporate governance and intranet/extranet capabilities	4	No	No
Mahadevan (2000)	Value stream, revenue stream, logistical stream	3	No	No
Gordijn et al. (2001)	Actors, market segments, value offering, value activity, stakeholder network, value interfaces, value ports and value exchanges	8	No	No
Linder and Cantrell (2001)	Pricing model, revenue model, channel model, commerce process model, internet-enabled commerce relationship, organizational form and Value proposition	8	No	Some
Chesbrough and Rosenbaum (2000)	Value proposition, target markets, internal value chain structure, cost structure and profit model, value network and competitive strategy	6	No	No
Gartner (2003)	Market offerings, competencies, core technology investments, and bottom line	4	No	Some
Hamel (2001)	Core strategy, strategic resources, value network and customer interface	4	No	No
Petrovic et al. (2001)	Value model, resource model, production model, customer relations model, revenue model, capital model, and market model	7	No	No

(continued)

Table 2.1 (continued)

Source	Components	Number of components	Eco-system	Digital platform
Dubosson-Torbay et al.	Products, customer relationship, infrastructure and network of partners, and financial aspects	4	No	Some
Afuah and Tucci (2001)	Customer value, scope, price, revenue, connected activities, implementation, capabilities and sustainability	8	No	Some
Weill and Vitale (2001)	Strategic objectives, value proposition, resource sources, success factors, channels, core competencies, customer segments, and IT infrastructure	8	No	No
Applegate (2001)	Concept, capabilities and value	3	No	No
Amit and Zott (2001)	Transaction content, transaction structure and transaction governance	4	No	No
Alt and Zimmerman (2001)	Mission, structure, process, revenues, legalities and technology	6	No	No
Rayport and Jaworski (2001)	Value cluster, market space offering, resource system, and financial model	4	No	No
Bertz (2002)	Resources, sales, profits and capital	4	No	No
Hedman and Kalling (2003)	Value network, resources, capabilities, revenue and pricing, competitors, output, management	7	Some	No
Chesbrough (2003)	Customer, value network, capabilities, revenue and pricing, cost, strategy	6	Some	No
Rappa (2004)	Types: Brokerage, advertising, infomediary, merchant, manufacturer (direct), affiliate, community, subscription, utility	9	Some	No
Stanoevska-Slabeva and Hoyer (2005)	Features of specific product, features of specific medium, customers, value chain, financial flow, goods and services, societal environment	7	No	No
Osterwalder and Pignuer (2009)	Customer segments, value propositions, channels, customer relationships, revenue streams, key resources, key activities, key partnerships, cost structures	9	Some	No

(continued)

Table 2.1   (continued)

Source	Components	Number of components	Eco-system	Digital platform
Al-Debei and Avison (2010)	Value proposition, value architecture, value finance, value network (integrated approach)	4	Yes	No

Adapted from Morris et al. op. cit. and Schafer et al. op. cit.

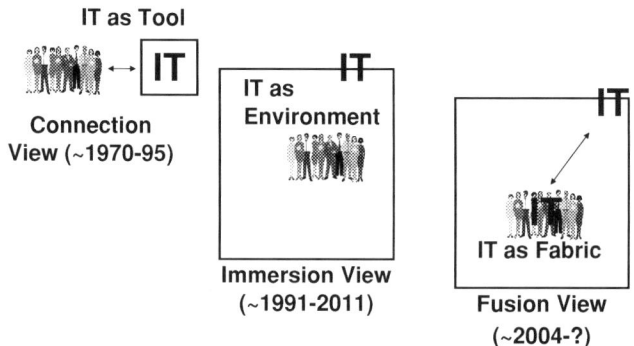

Fig. 2.2   Changing role of technology in business

into one fabric—it no longer makes sense to talk about information technology as a tool or environment that is kept at arm's length from business activities (El Sawy 2003). To theorize about new business models and by adding a few "digital" features to the theory would lead to what we call the "horseless carriage" fallacy. That term for the first automobiles constrained the imagination and blinded inventors to the fact that the new design challenge was fundamentally different than the old. We realize that a theory of digital business models and digital service must integrate the distinct attributes of digital business ecosystems from the get-go (Yoo et al. 2010). There are at least three such attributes: time compression, turbulence, and new architectures.

2.3 New Architectures

Digital business ecosystems feature not only idiosyncratic technological architectures (Yoo et al. 2010) but also important new interorganizational business architectures. Responding to the velocity and turbulence of the environment, and taking advantages of the affordances of digital technology, firms and groups of firms have been prolific in establishing *digital platforms* for the combination of technologies and the delivery of services (Gawer and Cusumano 2008). Platforms are standards or architectures that allow modular substitution of complementary assets (West 2003). Taking advantage of the digital affordance of modularity, platforms enable firms to focus their attention (and innovation) on one part of a system at a time, and to assemble those parts—whether they are products or activities—into a variety of configurations. As business models have become more digital, firm capabilities themselves have become more modular, more easily connectable, and more conveniently shareable. In prior decades it might have taken a formal alliance and a joint venture to make one firm's technology compatible with another's, but today, riding on rails of application programming interfaces (APIs) and broadband fiber optics, we can "mash up" digital services like Google's maps and Facebook's social newsfeed in no time and on a shoestring budget. Digital business ecosystems enable the possibility of combining capabilities across boundaries into innovative new offerings and solutions to create and capture value (Schlagwein and Schoder 2011).

Chapter 3
VISOR: A Unified Framework for Business Modeling in the Evolving Digital Space

The scientific objectives of this project are to advance our theoretical understanding of the structure of business models for digital platforms by devising a unified framework that brings together multiple elements and underlying drivers. This will allow us to better understand current and future business models, and to help the creation and categorization of a business model repository that researchers can continuously contribute to over time. This will also facilitate analyzing, from a more theoretical approach, the effects of disruptions and game changers. Understanding the theoretical structure of digital business models will also enable us to map the likely evolution of business models for the future.

3.1 Conceptual Development for Digital Business Models: Precursors to Design Theory

Design theories provide a useful vehicle for theory structure when designing artifacts which are enabled by digital platforms such as information systems and business models. Information systems design theory was developed by (Walls et al. 1992; 2004) and focused on theory building and theory testing for the design product and the design process. Each of those constitutes of several components. On the design product side, a set of meta-requirements that describe the class of goals to which the theory applies is determined. The term "meta-requirements" rather than simply requirements was used because a design theory does not address a single problem but rather a class of problems. The second component on the product side is a meta-design which describes a class of artifacts hypothesized to meet the meta-requirements. Again, the concept of "meta-design" is used because a design theory does not address the design of a specific artifact (e.g., the Executive Information System at XYZ Corporation) but a class of artifacts (e.g., all Executive Information Systems). A third component is a set of kernel theories

O. A. El Sawy and F. Pereira, *Business Modelling in the Dynamic Digital Space*, SpringerBriefs in Digital Spaces, DOI: 10.1007/978-3-642-31765-1_3, © The Author(s) 2013

Table 3.1 Components of an information system design theory (ISDT)

Design product	
1. Meta-requirements	Describes the class of goals to which the theory applies
2. Meta-design	Describes a class of artifacts hypothesized to meet the meta-requirements
3. Kernel theories	Theories from natural or social sciences governing design requirements
4. Testable design product hypotheses	Used to test whether the meta-design hypotheses satisfies the meta-requirements
Design process	
1. Design method	A description of procedure(s) for artifact construction
2. Kernel theories	Theories from natural or social sciences governing design process itself
3. Testable design process hypotheses	Used to verify whether the design hypotheses method results in an artifact which is consistent with the meta-design

from natural or social sciences that govern design requirements. The final component is a set of testable design process hypotheses that can be used to verify whether the meta-design satisfies the meta-requirements.

On the design process side there are several components of a design theory. The first component is a design method that describes procedures for artifact construction. A second component is a set of kernel theories from the natural or social sciences governing the design process itself. These kernel theories may be different from those associated with the design product. The final component is a set of testable design process hypotheses that can be used to verify whether or not the design method results in an artifact that is consistent with the meta-design. Table 3.1 and Fig. 3.1 (both from Walls et al. 2004) respectively show the components of an information system design theory and the relationships among these components.

In order to apply design theory to digital business models, there would be a requirement to construct and test such theories for classes of business models, rather than instances of business models. Thus, we believe we cannot a generic design theory for digital business models as we could not have a generic design theory for all classes of information systems. Thus, one could build design theories for each of executive information systems, knowledge management systems, transaction processing systems, customer relationship management systems, etcetera, as a class of information system. So, conceivably we could build design theories for different classed of digital business models. Similarly, we could build a design theory for long-tail business models, or social media business models, or open innovation business models, ex cetera. We could also use kernel theories from the social sciences such as consumer behavior, transaction cost theory of the firm, or organizational behavior. However, in order to do that we first need to develop a conceptual framework for articulation, development and better understanding o f the components of digital business models. In the information systems design theory field, we have agreement on what an information system is and what

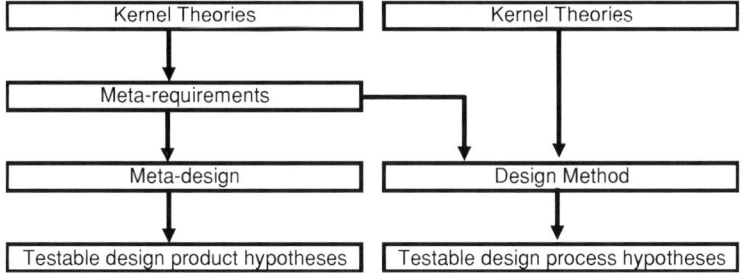

Fig. 3.1 Relationships between ISDT components

are its components. We agree that there is hardware, software, procedures, users, etc. and we understand each of those components, and what is means to have meta-requirements and design processes for different classes of information systems. In design theory for digital business models we are not at that stage yet and we need to define a conceptual framework for what the components of a digital business model. These are the prerequisite precursors to design theory.

3.2 A Unified Conceptual Framework for Components of Business Models

As Table 2.1 had illustrated, the articulated business models each have different components. However, as this project argues, the variously espoused components can be broadly classified into five categories, as captured by "Value proposition," "Interface," "Service Platform," "Organizing Model" and "Revenue Model" (VISOR). Figure 3.2 illustrates how the various components from a sample of the business models could be re-categorized into these five broad categories.

Thus, the VISOR[1] model attempts to integrate the different approaches in business model development, as well as to address unaddressed key elements such as the user experience and interface factors. While these factors are not explicitly recognized in most of the approaches as summarized in Table 2.1, they figure prominently in many theories of diffusion of innovations (Fife and Pereira 2005). At its core, a good business model must answer the age-old questions, as Peter Drucker is often quoted as asking, "Who is the customer? And what does the customer value? … How do we make money in this business? What is the underlying economic logic that explains how we can deliver value to the customers at an appropriate cost? (Mageretta 2002)".

---

[1] The VISOR Model was formulated by Omar El-Sawy et al. while Director of Research at CTM, and Professor of Information and Operations Management, Marshall School of Business, University of Southern California.

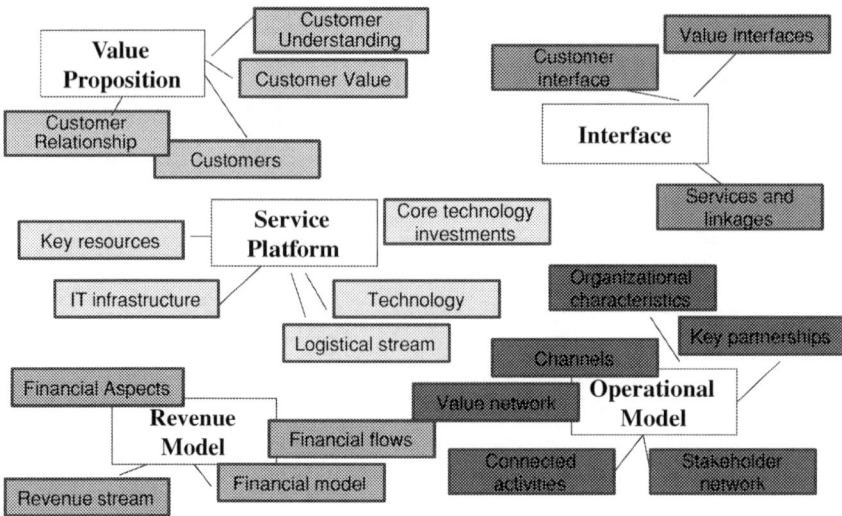

Fig. 3.2 Categorizing business model components

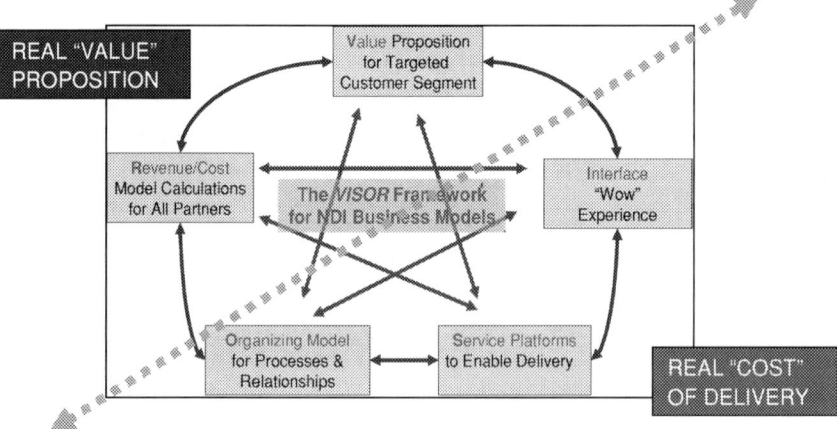

Fig. 3.3 The VISOR model

In this respect, then the VISOR Model, as illustrated in Fig. 3.3, defines how a firm responds to a customer need, latent or established, thus creating and delivering the greatest value to the customer, in a profitable and sustainable manner, and, as such, optimizes costs to value creation. Thus, from the VISOR perspective, a successful business model is one that is able to align the respective components of the VISOR model so as to deliver the greatest value proposition that maximize the willingness to pay on the part of its target consumers, on the one hand, with the ability to minimize the real cost (tangible and intangible) of the provision of these services, the latter being achieved through the optimal mix of interface experience, service platforms and the organizing model.

Many researchers in the fields of strategy, e-commerce, and entrepreneurship have promoted frameworks for business model development. They differ slightly, but the common thread is that they begin with the question "What value are we providing to the customer?" and end with "How are we going to make a profit doing that?" In the unique environment of the NDI, we believe that this process requires five key steps:

3.2.1 Value Proposition

Value proposition addresses why particular customer segments would value an enterprise's products and services and be willing to pay a premium price for them. The willingness to pay is a direct function of whether these applications provide "value creation" in that they satisfy an unmet latent end-user demand, or "value substitution" in that they provide only an alternative means for end-users to access an existing application or service.

Examples from other models:

- *Value proposition*, that is, the value created for users by the offering based on the technology (Chesbrough and Rosenbaum 2001)
- Value Propositions Building Block describes the bundle of products and services that create value for a specific Customer Segment (Osterwald and Piguer 2009)
- Customer value—customers would buy a product from a firm only if the product offers them something of value other products do not have… can take the form of differentiated or low cost products/services (Afuah and Tucci 2001).

The business modeler must identify the value provided to the ultimate customer or end user, even if the firm is part of a multi-firm value chain and doesn't reach the consumer directly. The key tension here is between the broad definition of the customer base, and the specificity of the value proposition. For example, a service like television broadly-defined has many different customers, who receive many different types of value. If you wish to reach all of them, then value must be understood generally as "access to favorite shows" or even "entertainment". By focusing on a narrow customer segment, however, value can be defined more precisely: for example, television allows *sports fans* to see a game live rather than hearing about it later. A more precise specification of the value proposition means reducing your focus to a smaller set of potential customers, but possibly satisfying that group more than any other business does.

3.2.2 Interface

The success of delivery of a product or service is heavily predicated on the user interface experience in terms of ease of use, simplicity, convenience, and positive energy, and should generate an extraordinary or "wow" experience.

New technologies are defined by affordances and limitations. Often, a business modeler in the NDI is asking, how do the unique characteristics of some new interface, such as a smart tablet, enable or inhibit the delivery of a specific type of value. For example, we might be developing a business model for a mobile television service. We know that the affordances of mobility include spatiality, temporality, and contextuality (Lee and Benbasat 2004). The limitations of mobility include a small screen, inconvenient input, and limited battery power. We might conclude that mobility enhances the value proposition of television for sports fans, because it ensures that they *won't miss* the live broadcast of a game no matter where they are, but it has a reduced value proposition for movie viewers, who would rather watch a film on the big screen at home than see a movie *right now*.

3.2.3 Service Platforms

IT platforms that enable, shape, and support the business processes and relationships that are needed to deliver the products and services, as well as improve the value proposition.

The term *platform or technology platform* describes a technical architecture that allows compatible complements to use it, e.g. an operating system (Gawer 2009; Schlagwein et al. 2010). A platform could be centered around a central technology or "keystone" (Iansiti and Levien 2004). The platform leader (Gawer and Cusumano 2002) manages a group of cooperating firms (Mikkola and Skjøtt-Larsen 2006) around that technology. The platforms leader enables other firms to build complementary products and services (Parker and Van Alstyne 2008).

Services in the NDI depend on technology infrastructures, and therefore an NDI business cannot be modeled without awareness of platform ecosystems.

Platforms define the "playing field" upon which partners collaborate, value is assembled, and customers access and discover a value proposition. Platforms create unique network externalities; Google's Android platform offers powerful technological APIs for search, mapping, and communication; Apple's IOS platform offers attractive interfaces and a polished, streamlined way to package and sell a service; Blackberry's Proprietary OS platform attracts a lucrative customer segment eager for business-related services. Platforms are constantly evolving and competing, and an important strategic choice is which platform you fit into, or whether and how you work across platforms. Key tensions include the ability of a platform to meet your technical requirements, and the appropriateness of its customer base to your value proposition.

Examples from other models

- The logistical stream addresses various issues related to the design of the supply chain for the business (Mahaderan 2000).

3.2.4 Organizing Model

Describes how an enterprise or a set of partners will organize business processes, value chains, and partner relationships to effectively and efficiently deliver products and services.

The NDI is a turbulent field that works more like an ecosystem than a traditional value chain. Major players compete and cooperate simultaneously. Much more than in traditional industries like auto manufacturing, the selection and configuration of partners may change with each new venture, and is a strategically important part of a business model. Business modelers must understand the venture's dependencies on other firms. To participate in an ecosystem is to be dependent upon "keystone" and "dominator" firms, making a venture sensitive to changes in their technology or market position, but also opening doors to partnerships with other firms in that ecosystem. In developing the organizing model, the firm's competitive instinct may be balanced with an imperative to cooperate for the health of the overall ecosystem.

Allee (2000) states that a value network generates economic value through complex dynamic exchanges between one or more enterprises, customers, suppliers, strategic partners and the community. In our opinion, actors in value network include the focal firm and its affiliated companies, and all the organizations and individuals which affect the focal firm's value creation activities. The relations among actors include tangible flows like products, service and profit, and intangible ones like knowledge, emotion and influence. Actually, these flows are value flows formed by value activities like value creation, value delivery and value capture. Actors are linked by these value flows and constitute network structure.

Examples from other Business Models

- Value Network—value network generates economic value through complex dynamic exchanges between one or more enterprises, customers, suppliers, strategic partners and the community… The relations among actors include tangible flows like products, service and profit, and intangible ones like knowledge, emotion and influence (Allee 2000).
- Key resources—Assets such as people, technology, products, facilities, equipment channels and brand required to deliver the value proposition to the targeted customer (Johnson et al. 2008).

3.2.5 Revenue Model

In a good business model, the combination of the value proposition, the way that offerings are delivered, and the investments in IT platforms are such that revenues exceed costs and attractive for all partners.

Finally, the business modeler must ask, "How do we make money doing this?" In the NDI, it's important to conduct ongoing research into user preferences and the prices that consumers are willing to pay. These may change as different user groups such as early adopters, mass market, and laggards start using the technology, and they experiment with options. Often, the service platform and organizing model must be taken into account, and it can be a complex undertaking to find out how each partner in a value chain can profit. Actually collecting the money may be a challenge, too, for services delivered online by micropayments.

Examples from Other Business Models:

- The *cost structure* and *profit potential* of producing the offering, given the value proposition and value chain structure chosen (Chesbrough and Rosenbaum 2005)
- The revenue streams... represents the cash a company generates from each Customer Segment (costs must be subtracted from revenues to create earnings) (Osterwalder and Pigneur 2010)
- The revenue stream is a plan for assuring revenue generation for the business (Mahadevan 2000).

Dynamics of the Digital Eco-system

We have shown in Chap. 1 how value is co-created, converted, and captured through a variety of players in the digital business ecosystem. We have shown above what the components of a digital business model can be conceived to be. Figure 3.4 shows the relationship between the two. Digital business model designs can only make sense in the context of the dynamics of the digital business ecosystem in which they are in and their accompanying game changers. These conditions will suggest alternative business model designs that match the environment, and best contribute to the creation, conversion and capture of value. Thus, digital business models and the dynamics of digital business ecosystems are highly interdependent. We shall explore more of those interdependencies in Chaps. 4 and 5.

3.3 Articulating the VISOR Components

While we emphasize that each component is equally important, if we do little re-arranging, we articulate the five business model drivers in the NDI according to the acronym VISOR: value proposition, interfaces, service platforms, organizing models, and revenue/cost model. Each of these drivers can be fleshed out as a list of *strategic choices* that are made as part of the business modeling process.

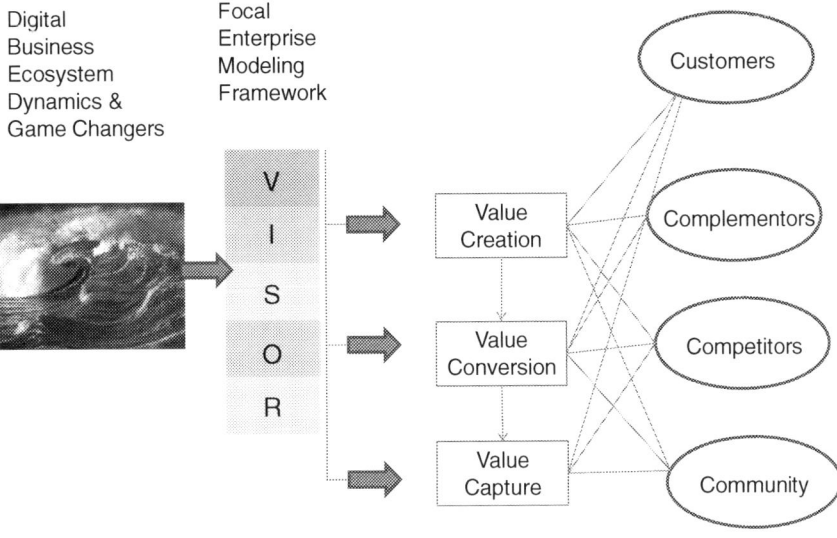

Fig. 3.4 Using the VISOR framework in context of dynamics of the digital business ecosystem

3.3.1 Value Proposition

The value proposition addresses why particular customer segments would value an enterprise's products and services and be willing to pay a price for them. Thus, the value proposition is the sum total of all the benefits the customer derives from the product or service. As such, it is a measure of the "value creation" that the products or services provide to the customers and thus must satisfy an unmet latent end-user demand. It can be defined in terms several questions that need to be answered:

- What "job" are we doing? (Precise is better: i.e. "I don't want an MP3 player, I want *music*")
- For whom are we doing it? (Understand target customers and their unique needs.)
- Why is it valuable to our customers? (Better quality? Lower cost? More precisely fits their need? Reaches customers who can't access competitive offerings?)

From the VISOR perspective, value creation can be defined by the following descriptors in Table 3.2.

Table 3.2 Descriptors of the Value Proposition

Descriptor	Explanation	Method of assessment
Compelling	The extent to which a product or service vividly addresses a need for the customer	Likelihood of consumption or acquisition
Cohort	The number of customers in a particular market segment, who view the product or service as addressing or providing a need	Size of market niche
Complementarity	The extent to which the product or service accentuates or improves a product or service that a customer currently owns or uses	The number of other existing products or services that are interdependent in their consumption
Co-creatibility	The extent to which customers can add or alter features of the digital products or service	The number of variations that could be generated by customers

3.3.2 Interfaces

The interface is the interaction (interconnection) between the customer experience and the service platform. It includes both hardware and software. It is the link between the qualitative and experiential nature of the value proposition and the physical infrastructure that delivers it. New interfaces such as mobile phones, smart phone operating systems, social media, and now tablet PCs offer new avenues to deliver digital products and services. They create the possibility of new business models for old products and services, and for new product offerings.

The interface addresses the following questions:

• Do the *affordances* of new interfaces enhance our value proposition? (example: social networking helps music customers discover new and better music through their friends; mobility affords *social presence* by being aware of location and time)
• Do new interfaces help us deliver a more "precise" value to customers?
• Do the *limitations* of new interfaces detract from our value proposition (example: how satisfying is TV on a tiny mobile device?)
• How can we use multiple interfaces in conjunction (example: connecting your TIVO to your mobile and your PC...)

From a VISOR perspective, the Interface can be described in the following way in Table 3.3

Table 3.3 Descriptors of the Interface

Descriptor	Explanation	Method of assessment
Functionality	The range of types of interactions of the interface and its ease of use	Ability to access range of service platforms, and supports multiplicity of tasks
Form factor	The aesthetics of the interface	Customer perception
Fluidity	Provides the customer with flexibility, intimacy, personalization, and control	Ease and extent of customization
Forgiveness	The ability of the interface to automatically undo any user error	Extent of error correction and adaptiveness

3.3.3 Service Platform

IT platforms that enable, shape, and support the business processes and relationships that are needed to deliver the products and services, as well as improve the value proposition. Services in the NDI depend on technology infrastructures, and therefore an NDI business cannot be modeled without awareness of platform ecosystems.

As discussed above in Chap. 2, platforms are constantly evolving and competing, and an important strategic choice is which platform you fit into, or whether and how enterprises work across platforms. In deciding which platforms to chose, enterprises must answer the following questions:

- Which platform(s) offer the best opportunities and capabilities to deliver our value proposition to our target customers, and execute our revenue model?
- Will we bet big on one platform becoming dominant, or hedge our bets with multiple platforms? Does it make sense for us to develop a platform of our own?
- If we're targeting multiple platforms, how should we adapt our offering to take advantage of the features and the target customers that use each?

Service platforms in the VISOR framework are captured through the following descriptors in Table 3.4

3.3.4 Organizing Model

The digital eco-system is turbulent, and unlike traditional value chains, is characterized major players competing and cooperating simultaneously. Much more than in traditional industries like auto manufacturing, the selection and structure of partnerships may change with each new venture, and is a strategically important component of a business model.

As stated above, the organizing model describes how an enterprise or a set of partners will organize business processes, value chains, and partner relationships

Table 3.4 Descriptors of the Service Platform

Descriptor	Explanation	Method of assessment
Architecture	The topology of the hardware and software that enables the service	Closed/proprietary or open standards
Agnosticity	Whether the platform supports different operating systems	Depends on type of technology environment or the need for external APIs
Acquisition	Addresses the question of whether to build, or piggy-back on existing technology infrastructures	Availability of existing platforms able to deliver product or services
Access	Defines the community which would be able to access the service	Continuum from walled garden, to totally open

to effectively and efficiently deliver products and services. In the new digital eco-system, the enterprise can partner with complementors, competitors, customers and even the community

Some key questions that the organizing model must addresses:

• What other kinds of services are needed to deliver this value (ex: a mobile TV service needs content producers, device designers, a network provider)?
• Who are the best partners to work with, given the value proposition, revenue model, target customers, target platforms, and desired interfaces?
• Who will likely compete with us if we don't include them? How will power and decision-making be controlled, or shared, in this venture?
• Are we dependent on our partners more than they depend on us, or vice versa?

In the VISOR Framework, the Organizing Model can be described using the four descriptors in Table 3.5.

3.3.5 Revenue Model

In a good business model, the combination of the value proposition, the way that offerings are delivered, and the investments in IT platforms are such that revenues exceed costs and attractive for all partners.

Some questions that have to be answered when developing the revenue model include:

• What structure of pricing should be employed?
• What is the revenue sharing percentage among partners?
• At what point will the revenues exceed costs to make the investment profitable?

In the VISOR Framework, he revenue model is described in Table 3.6.

Table 3.5 Descriptors of the Organizing Model

Descriptor	Explanation	Method of assessment
Processes	The design of the core business processes that are necessary to deliver and support the digital product or service	Determination of the effectiveness of key business processes such as new product introduction, order management, customer support...
Partnerships	Quality of business relationships with go-to-market partners for service	Partnerships can be assessed in terms of formality, exclusivity, and expected durability of relationships
Pooling	Pooling refers to the necessity of combining complementary assets or capabilities of different partners to be able provide customer value	Extent of synergy and complementarity on various resources (talent, technology,...)
Project management	Coordination of effort across different partners for launch of service, and continuing service offering	Probability of success given complexity of task and relationships

Table 3.6 Descriptors of the Revenue Model

Descriptor	Explanation	Method of assessment
Pricing	Structure of pricing mechanism	Type of pricing: subscription, pay-as-you-go, advertising, all you can eat, micropayments,...
Partner revenue sharing	How revenue is shared among partners who are bringing the joint offering to market	Distribution proration among partners
Product cost structure	Direct and indirect cost of key resources required	Product margins and cost assessment
Potential volume	How much demand is expected in target market segment	Expected number of "units" sold in specified time period

3.4 Design Theory and the VISOR Conceptual Framework

As we have discussed in Sect. 3.1, in applying design theory for digital business we need to first define a conceptual framework for what the components of a digital business model. These are the prerequisite precursors to design theory. The above section presents VISOR as such a conceptual framework. As an illustration, Table 3.7 suggests how specific classes of digital business models could be designed using the components of VISOR. However, Table 3.7 provides only a

Table 3.7 Designing Digital Business Models Using the VISOR Components

	VISOR components				
	Value proposition	Interface	Service platform	Organizing model	Revenue model
Design product					
Meta-requirements	Quality of life improvements; search costs reduction	Reduction in complexity in use	Open standards	New product introduction; improved customer support;	Subscription model; micro-payments
Meta-design	Market segmentation; Consumption behavior	Voice-activated systems; RFID systems; Sensor grids	Open system platforms; network effects	Decentralized structure	Cross-subsidization; bundling
Kernel theories	Consumer behavior theory; rational expectation; decisions under uncertainty	Diffusion of innovation, TAM model	Metcalf's Law; Beckstrom's Law;	Transaction costs theory; organizational theory; disintermediation theory	Constrained maximization
Testable design product hypotheses	Specified to unique class of business model being designed, and in terms of interaction between components				
Design process					
Design method	Dependent on specific digital product or service being offered, choice of interface, service platform, organizing model and revenue model (VISOR) descriptors selected				
Kernel theories	Depends on the specific digital product or service being offered, and the VISOR descriptors (interface, service platform, organizing model and revenue model)] selected as key differentiators				
Testable design process hypotheses	Depends on the specific digital product or service being offered				

sample of the design theory requirements for creating a specific class of digital business models in the context of the VISOR conceptual framework, and is not meant to be exhaustive.

Chapter 4
A View Through the VISOR Lens

This chapter analyses three case studies of digital business models through the VISOR framework. We pick these companies as they are in relatively mature industries (athletic shoes, car rental, and healthcare) and articulate how they have changed their business models by taking advantage of digital platforms in an evolving environment. The VISOR framework helps to systematically examine and assess the many facets of those digital models allowing better analysis and an articulated unified framework that managers from different functional areas can discuss with a common language whether they are from marketing, operations, technology, or finance. In general, the three cases illustrate how these companies have been innovative and capitalized on new technological developments:

(i) Expanding the eco-system and partnering with companies outside the traditional eco-system
(ii) Utilizing the service platform to build more formal relationships with partners so as to be able to deliver bundled offerings
(iii) Enhancing the customer experience through improvements in the interface.

4.1 Case Study: Nike+

Nike, Inc. was founded, in 1964, as Blue Ribbon Sports by a University of Oregon track athlete and his coach, and began as a distributor of athletic shoes made by other companies. Since the emergence of its Nike product line in the early 1970s, it has become the world's leading manufacturer of athletic footwear and apparel for a wide range of sports. From a business model perspective, the value proposition of physical goods, like sneakers, is the sum total of all the benefits the customer derives from using the product or service. Historically then, managers were trained to assume that competitive success accrued to making the highest-quality product. Nike's original business model is represented in Table 4.1. However Nike has had

O. A. El Sawy and F. Pereira, *Business Modelling in the Dynamic Digital Space*,
SpringerBriefs in Digital Spaces, DOI: 10.1007/978-3-642-31765-1_4,
© The Author(s) 2013

Table 4.1 Conventional
shoe apparel business model

Value proposition	High quality, athletic footwear and apparel
Interface	Store-front, possibly catalog and on-line ordering
Service platform	Corporate intranet with limited access to partners
Organizing model	Traditional logistic-supply chain
Revenue model	Sale of footwear and athletic apparel

a different perspective and it always focused on understanding that the value proposition of its customers was subjective: basketball players realize value when they can jump higher; sprinters realize value when they can run faster; marathoners realize value when they can endure longer. By paying attention to the customer experience of value, and designing its shoes and other products accordingly, Nike prospered.

4.1.1 Capitalizing on a New Organizing Model

Nike continually experimented with new value offerings. For runners, Nike realized that two important parts of the customer's running experience were motivation and performance feedback, and it sought ways to serve these needs, even tinkering with the idea of a "smart shoe". In 1987, it introduced a tentative product called the Nike Monitor, a bulky but wearable device that would use sonar to detect a runner's speed and distance. Initially, the Nike Monitor wasn't a success but over the years Nike added sports watches, heart rate monitors, and other gear directed at the same type of value experience: letting runners know how they were doing. Around 2004, Nike engineers began to notice that more and more joggers were running with music, and that the Apple iPod specifically was their device of choice. The main roadblock to selling a "smart shoe" or a device like a heart rate monitor had been that it was difficult to get performance data off the equipment and into a form that the customer can use, but with the iPod, here was a digital device that runners carried with them on every run and manually synced up with their internet-capable computer on a regular basis. Nike quickly realized that running, music, and performance data could be combined with the use of the iPod for a superior customer experience that none of their competitors could match, and began developing the Nike+ system with Apple's help.

Nike+ is simple. The customer purchases a cheap sensor (an accelerometer) and inserts it into the sole of a compatible Nike running shoe. The sensor transmits data wirelessly to the runner's iPod, so that when he presses the "start" button, the iPod begins recording the time, speed, and distance of the run. When the user syncs the iPod with his home computer, that data is uploaded to the Nike+ website where he can see his performance tracked over time and even share the data with friends. Even though the system really only captures two variables, time and speed, the ability to track one's own performance improvement over time and compare it to goals has proven incredibly valuable to customers.

When Nike+ users started uploading their personal statistics to the Internet, funny things began happening. Runners were not only interested in viewing their own performance, but also in sharing it with friends, and seeing what others in the community were doing. The result was a powerful new avenue for social motivation to go running. Users could form running clubs to train together with friends in different places, could challenge rivals to friendly competitions, and could participate in virtual events with the whole community. Beginning in August 2008, Nike organized its first virtual 10 K race, with 800,000 runners in cities all around the world running independently or in groups and uploading their statistics to the Nike+ web community. Other such events have followed.

Because the Nike+ service is offered for free, and iPod sales accrue to Apple, we don't know exactly how profitable Nike+ has been for Nike. The sales of the shoe-sensors are probably a tiny fraction of Nike's overall revenue, but Nike credits Nike+ with building the brand and growing its market share for running shoes every year since its launch. Customers buy Nike shoes not necessarily because they are superior to other brands (competition in this regard is very intense) but because the value-in-use they experience from Nike+ is significantly greater than the value they could realize with another brand's shoe and no Nike+. So far, only Adidas has developed a similar offering combining a "smart shoe" with an online service, and it remains to be seen how the competition will develop.

Since launching Nike+, Nike has continued to introduce new features on top of the basic Nike+ service. The user's online presence now works in conjunction with social networking platforms such as Facebook and Twitter; as each uploaded run is seen by friends, this contributes to the motivation of the runner as well as to rivals in his network. The Apple iPhone and a Nike wristband have been developed as alternatives to the iPod for receiving the shoe-sensor data. An experimental mapping feature is currently being rolled out, integrating Google's maps (freely available through an open API) and the iPhone's GPS capability, so that users can map their running routes. Apple has also worked with Nike to develop the music-related aspect of the service. Nike+ now allows users to designate "powersongs" for extra motivation during a difficult run, and to share these choices socially. Over the course of running some 330 million miles, Nike's customers have uploaded massive amounts of personal-performance data to the Nike + website, and it remains to be seen what other uses can be found for this data. Health experts in particular are optimistic about how this cornucopia of vital statistics data might be potentially used in a whole new set of digital health care services, once the privacy issues are worked out.

4.1.2 Nike+ in the Digital Eco-System

Figure 4.1 illustrates the narrative of the Nike + case study in the context of digital services and digital business models, capabilities, configurations, and

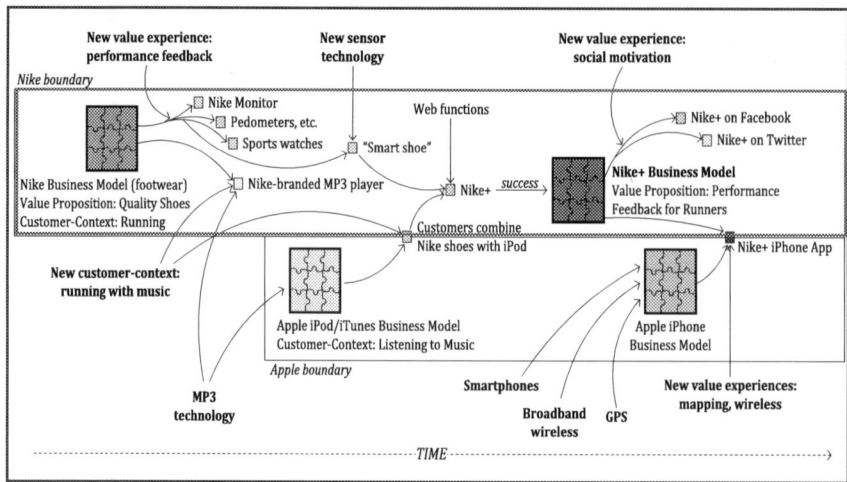

Fig. 4.1 Nike and expansion of the eco-system. (By incorporating new digital technologies into its traditional business model, Nike has been able to expand its ecosystem and provide new digital services: (i) Nike's use of sensor technology embedded in its "smart shoe," and its use of the iPod as a wireless receiver, through its partnership with Apple, has allowed Nike to expand its customer value proposition into the Health field; (ii) By embedding sensor technology into sports-wear that would allow monitoring of body vital statistics, Nike is positioning itself to potentially develop partnerships with traditional health care providers)

customer-contexts. Chronologically, beginning on the left, we see that the established Nike footwear business model was the jumping-off point for several new service innovations intended to offer customers the value experience of performance feedback, but many of these service offerings were temporary, experimental, and either failed or remain ancillary to Nike's main business.

About the same time, the concept of people running or exercising while listening to music became increasingly important. Nike tried offering an MP3 player (drawing on a new technology capability) as a service offering for this customer-context, but Apple was so successful in the MP3 ecosystem that customers themselves began two service offerings together: Nike shoes and Apple's iPod. Recognizing the iPod's dot-connecting potential for an experimental "smart shoe" idea, Nike integrated the smart shoe and iPod with a website to form a complete Nike+ system. At some point in time, Nike+ graduated from "experiment" status to become a digital business model in its own right. Note that this does not mean that we think the footwear business disappeared; a firm may have more than one concurrent business model. The success of Nike+ in tweaking its business model can be gleaned from the new service innovations, including Facebook, Twitter, and iPhone applications.

Figure 4.1, delineates the traditional "boundaries" of Nike and Apple. This diagram illustrates that the most interesting service offerings draw upon a mix of capabilities developed internally (e.g. the Nike+ web functions), technologies from outside the ecosystem (MP3, new sensors, GPS), and bits and pieces of other

Table 4.2 NIKE+: expanding the digital ecosystem for sports apparel

	Traditional business model	NIKE+
Value proposition	High quality, athletic footwear and apparel	Integrated digital and sensor technology to monitor body vital signs in athletic apparel
Interface	Store-front, possibly catalog and on-line ordering	Multi-modal: store-front, internet for online download sites, and mobile devices
Service platform	Corporate intranet with limited access to partners	Integrated with partners
Organizing model	Traditional logistic-supply chain	Partnerships with companies outside sports apparel eco-system
Revenue model	Sale of footwear and athletic apparel	Sale of footwear and athletic apparel as well as partnership revenue sharing

companies' business models accessed through digital platforms or exclusive alliances. What is defined as the "value proposition" in one of Apple's digital business model is treated as a "capability" in the Nike+ digital business model. Other intrusions from outside Nike that affect the direction of digital service innovation are new customer-contexts, emerging technologies, and customer demands for new types of value (Table 4.2).

Thus, in summary, companies that continually experiment with adding new service offerings that build on its established business model, as new technologies become available and as new ways for customers to realize value in context are discovered. It also shows a company that freely draws upon capabilities from other companies' in the eco-system (notably Apple's) to assemble its uniquely valuable configurations. It was a winning configuration, rather than any particular component technology, that allowed one experimental service to mature into a new digital business model.

4.2 Case 2 Study: Humana

One example of a strong innovator in the health care arena is Humana, a benefits solutions company, offering an array of health and supplemental benefit products for employer groups, government benefit programs, and individuals. Headquartered in Kentucky, Humana provides health insurance benefits to over 11.5 million customers in all 50 states, including to beneficiaries of Medicare, Medicaid, and Military insurance programs. Its core business model is to provides health insurance benefits under health maintenance organization (HMO), private fee-for-service (PFFS) and preferred provider organization (PPO) plans, as shown in Table 4.3. However, Humana is distinguished by a number of innovative new digital services it has developed in the past few years.

Guided by the vision of serving as a health information hub for its customers, Humana recognized that the missing piece of such a service was getting doctors to interact with a website for self-service. Humana CIO Bruce Goodman said in an

Table 4.3 Humana in non-
digital ecosystem

Value proposition	Health insurance and co-pay model
Interface	Traditional doctor-patient consultation
Service platform	Non-digital
Organizing model	Limited to medical supply vendors
Revenue model	Insurance premiums

interview with the Wall Street Journal: "The difficulty was that a typical doctor's office has patients from dozens of different health plans. So, each health plan has various degrees of advancement in terms of providing Web capability, right? And then the doctors would have to train their staff, which tends to have a fairly high turnover in the front office, to use all of those different systems. So, we got to a certain point of adoption and we were having a hard time getting beyond that." To solve the problem, Humana had a conversation with a competitor, Blue Cross Blue Shield of Florida, and proposed the creation of a uniform web portal for all plan providers. The uniform portal would allow doctors to learn a single system and be able to access any patient's records, even those with small, local insurance companies. The web portal now covers 95 % of all patients in Florida and is expanding to other states. In terms of our framework, the portal is a new interface through which Humana reaches doctors to co-create valued services. Once it was in place, they were able to develop new service offerings, including clinical trans-actions like e-prescribing. These have been highly profitable, doing 600 million transactions and earning $70 million in revenue a year.

Goodman believes that the next big capabilities we need are for doctors to use electronic medical records and for patients to adopt personal electronic health records. Reflecting a service-dominant logic, he understands that these technolo-gies won't be adopted until patients and doctors are able to see that they can experience subjective value from them. "And frankly until you connect all the pieces and crunch it with data analytics, there isn't a lot of value to it. Part of [what will drive] adoption is getting everybody hooked up, and then generating action-able information that is useful to everybody in the system."

Instead of focusing on a future scenario in which all the puzzle pieces are already in place, though, Humana has kept up the pace with service innovations on a small scale. Its innovations in mobile games for health are examples of ways to get customers to happily sign up for electronic services that connect them to their insurance provider. In 2010 it launched the game Colorfall through the Apple iTunes AppStore. This game challenges the player to arrange cascading color tokens in the order of the rainbow spectrum; the physical challenge is that to get each color, the customer must find and photograph an object of that color. The value-in-use of this game is not only entertainment but also physical exercise and mental stimulation. A web-based game, FamScape, allows family members and friends to set exercise goals and challenge one another to meet them. The game can connect to third-party devices like pedometers that enable players to earn points for exercise. At this point it's not clear whether the games are earning money for Humana or whether they're just experiments, but at any rate Humana is using them to interface with new customers and certainly acquiring lots of potentially-valuable exercise data (much like Nike+) upon which future services could be built.

A new service offering geared toward getting doctors and patients more tightly integrated with the insurance company is Humana's "medical home" concept being tried out with Medicare Advantage customers in Florida. In the "medical home", doctors serve as "quarterbacks" for their elderly patients' whole lifestyles, using technology to manage exercise, weight, nutrition, prescriptions. The doctor serves as the communication hub for specialists and testing centers, with the goal of managing a patient's wellness instead of waiting for acute emergencies to drive a patient into the doctor's office. There is evidence that patients are experiencing substantial value from the medical home concept: hospital readmission rates are dropping; costs for ER visits, hospitalization and prescriptions are falling; blood sugar and cholesterol levels are more likely to be in the optimal ranges, and overall, patients are reporting happiness and satisfaction.

Humana is a profitable and growing company that stands to benefit from the expected industry consolidation as the American health care system changes in the near future. Part of its success is almost certainly due to its active and robust innovation efforts. We see in this case a company that embraces digital business model thinking. Not only does Humana perceive its entire business model, from the digital platforms that enable its service offerings to the subjective value that customers wish to experience, but it also thinks forward to future business models it would like to reach, and innovates step-by-step the new capabilities, platforms, and interfaces that it will need to get there.

4.2.1 Diagramming Humana

In our first narrative diagram of the Humana case study, Fig. 4.2, we observe some new phenomena unlike the Nike+ case. First, Humana is an actively-innovating company that appears to strike out into blue water from time to time. Its "medical home" concept, for example, builds on Humana's current business model and capitalizes on the popularity of video gaming and proliferation of mobile devices. On the other hand, innovative digital health-enhancing games like Colorfall and FamScape do draw on technology platforms from outside Humana's boundaries but do not really use any of Humana's existing resources; they are all new as far as the company is concerned.

We found that the shared portal that CIO Bruce Goodman discussed was a good example case for attempting to diagram coopetition—a phenomenon we identified as a necessity in digital business ecosystems. Humana and its competitors forged a new organizing model, a joint venture, to create a prototype web interface that would serve as a common platform for all of their digital services to doctors. At the time of Goodman's interview, the new web portal was well-established in one state and expanding nationwide. As it was a valuable and unique combination of capabilities with a serious value proposition to benefits providers and to doctors'

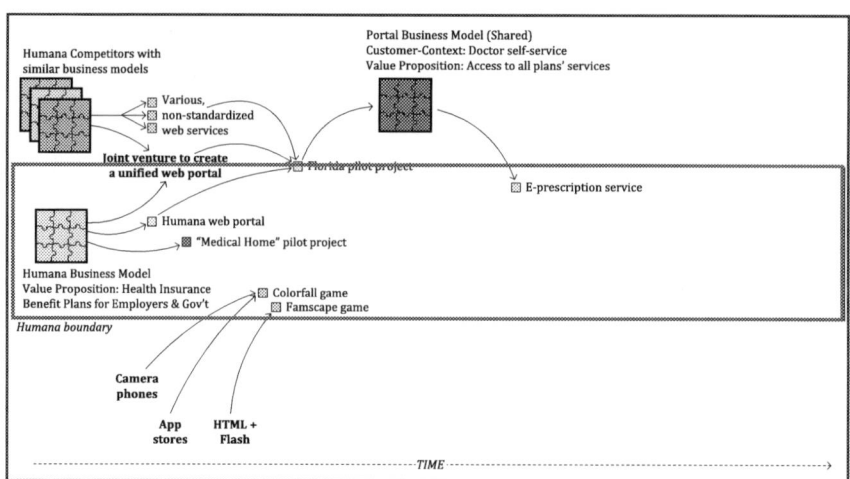

Fig. 4.2 Humana's expanded eco-system. (Figure 4.2 illustrates how Humana has capitalized on developments in digital technology to alter its business model and expand its eco-system by: (i) employing web-based services to provide a uniform portal for its partners, which in turn allowed Humana to provide new digital service offerings; (ii) working with game development companies to create mobile and web-based health monitoring games; (iii) developing the "medical home" concept for senior citizens through the use of new communication technologies)

offices, and was serving as a launch pad for new services, it had become a new digital business model. Although it was not owned by Humana, but shared, Humana was able to offer services of its own, like e-prescribing, upon the platform.

In order to make some sense of some of the disconnected service innovations we read about in the case, we tried an experiment with the diagram. Based on Goodman's comments about capabilities needed and future realization of value, we conjectured that Humana's digital service innovation is anchored by a vision of a *future* business model, and we added its logic to the diagram, Fig. 4.2. Viewed from right to left, it shows that each of Humana's innovations makes sense in terms of an envisioned business model. Bit by bit, Humana is working toward creating the envisioned customer-contexts (doctors accessing Humana's services by self-service web portals), capabilities (electronic medical records, which in turn need a value offering to get patients to adopt them), and configurations (the "medical home" vision) (Table 4.4). If our conjecture is correct, then we are observing a different way of motivating digital service innovation than was observed at Nike.

4.3 Case Study 3: Zipcar

It is very easy to notice the green Zipcar signs sprouting up in prime parking spaces at university campuse s all over the United States. This Boston-based upstart, founded in 2000, is now the dominant player in the nation's rapidly-

Table 4.4 Humana and tweaks in the business model

	Current	New model
Value proposition	Health insurance and co-pay model	Health insurance and co-pay model
Interface	Traditional doctor-patient consultation	Multimodal to support remote health consultation and monitoring
Service platform	Non-digital	Integrated with partners
Organizing model	Limited to medical supply vendors	Expansion of eco-system by partnering with gaming and entertainment companies
Revenue model	Insurance premiums	Insurance premiums and chronic disease avoidance

Table 4.5 A VISOR review of the traditional car rental business model

Value proposition	Rental of cars by mainly business travelers at transportation hubs, such as airports
Interface	Tele-phone or Internet reservation
Service platform	Corporate intranet with limited access
Organizing model	Limited partnerships with some hotel chains and travel agencies
Revenue model	Daily car rentals and optional insurance

growing "car sharing" market, and expanding by acquisitions into Western Europe. Car sharing is a new variation on the well-established business model of car rental. Instead of having cars available at airports and other transportation hubs, though, Zipcars are available mainly around universities and urban downtowns where apartment-dwellers who don't own cars may be found. And instead of renting cars by the day, Zipcars are rented by the hour. Beginning with a single lime-green Volkswagen Beetle in 2000, the company has grown to a fleet of more than 8,000 cars in 50 cities and on 150 college campuses, partly by acquisition and merger with rivals like Flexcar.

Although Zipcar provides an offering (cars) similar to traditional car-rental companies like Enterprise and Avis (Table 4.5), the value that customers realize is very different. Zipcar signs up customers as "members" and they pay a small annual fee for the right to access a car at any time they need one for rates as low as $8 per hour. With their membership fee, they are paying for "mobility when and where I need it"—in other words, the ability to occasionally drive somewhere without having to buy, garage, and maintain a car of their own. Zipcar has discovered a set of customers who aren't satisfied with the value proposition of public transit, yet who cannot reach traditional rental car agencies whose vehicles and staff are generally far from their apartment communities. The Zipcars are located in special reserved parking spaces that the company acquires in prime locations where members can easily hop in and go.

Careful examination shows that Zipcar has innovated far more than just a new customer segment and new payment model, though. One of the foundations of the business is an RFID transponder in each car that detects a member's "Zipcard" to lock and unlock the doors. This allows the cars to be rented nearly-spontaneously (reservations can be made minutes in advance by phone or through a website) without need of a human attendee. Each car also features an onboard computer that records mileage, hours of use, can locate the vehicle and can prevent it from starting in case of theft. These clever technologies draw on existing infrastructure—ubiquitous internet connectivity, broadband wireless networks, and GPS—to enable almost-entirely automated operations. In the back office, Zipcar has also developed a powerful fleet-management information system that allows them to manage reservations, analyze usage to identify traffic patterns and customer demand for cars, and optimize fueling and maintenance in their fleets.

Once established, Zipcar's basic IT proved to be the foundation for building additional functionalities and service offerings. One such offering is an iPhone application that allows members ("Zipsters") to locate an empty car by honking the horn remotely, and to unlock the doors by remote. Another is a service that allows customers to extend a reservation by sending a text message. But interestingly, Zipcar has also built on its embedded systems and fleet-management infrastructure to create another service for another type of customer: FastFleet by Zipcar offers the same fleet-management software to universities, corporations, and government agencies to manage their own fleets for efficient usage and maintenance. After a successful pilot project at a government agency in Washington, DC, the FastFleet service has been offered nationwide and successfully received.

4.3.1 Diagramming Zipcar

This case study gives us the opportunity to diagram the digital service innovation trajectory in a startup company, as illustrated in Fig. 4.3. Unlike Nike and Humana, Zipcar's story doesn't start with an established business model, but with a pilot project involving a single car. The experimental service began with most of the necessary parts of a digital business model already in place: some capabilities (the car), a configuration (a membership model with hourly rental rates), and most importantly, an innovative value proposition that created significant value to a certain intersection of customer and context. During the startup phase, a host of new capabilities were incorporated into a digital car-sharing service. Without these, Zipcar's business model would never have been possible. In a sense, this narrative is like Nike's, where we saw service innovation spurred by the emergence of new capabilities, but in another sense it is like Humana's, where innovators were actively trying to assemble the puzzle pieces of an envisioned, intended business model.

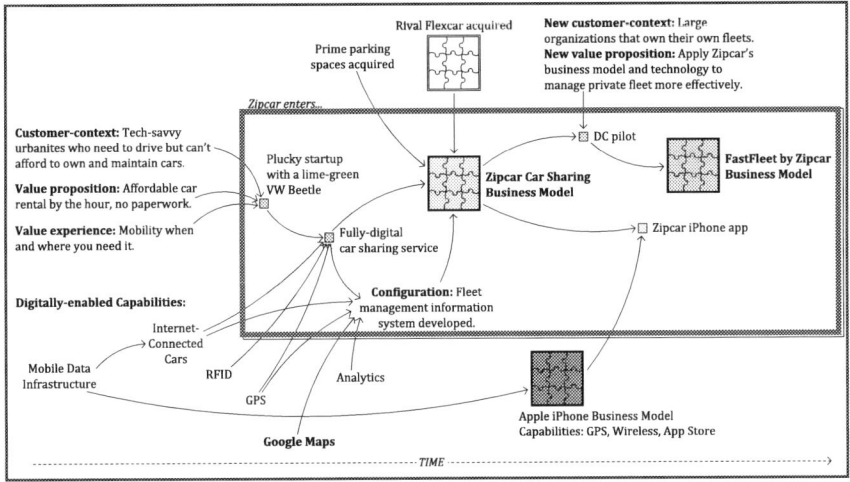

Fig. 4.3 Zipcars' ecosystem. (Zipcar has employed new wireless and communication technologies into the traditional business model of car rental agencies, and has thus created a new business model in this industry: (i) through the use of RPID transponders and GPS, it has "automated" the car-rental business; (ii) developed new partnerships with non-traditional players in the industry, such as parking companies)

Table 4.6 ZipCar and tweaks in the traditional car rental business model

	Traditional model	ZipCar
Value proposition	Rental of cars by mainly business travelers at transportation hubs, such as airports	Hourly rental of cars from decentralized locations for urban apartment dwellers who don't own cars
Interface	Tele-phone or internet reservation	Multimodal access and through wide area network
Service platform	Corporate intranet with limited access	Proprietary network with limited access
Organizing model	Limited partnerships with some hotel chains and travel agencies	Partnerships with universities and other entities
Revenue model	Daily car rentals and optional insurance	Membership fee and hourly rental of cars

We mark the point of establishment, where Zipcar went from being a digital service to a digital business model, around the time it merged with its rival Flexcar in 2007. That merger resulted in a basically settled digital infrastructure for the merged company, and established Zipcar's model as the one to imitate. To get to that point, Zipcar had acquired a couple of capabilities: prime parking spaces (which may or may not be seen as VRIN), and a very effective fleet management system. We would argue that this information system fits the description of "configuration" we used in explicating the digital business model framework: by creating cospecialization and complementarity between capabilities, this analytical and operational IT system makes Zipcar's combined capabilities more valuable than the sum of their parts (Table 4.6). We see that the fleet management system itself was spun off as an additional business model to serve the need of a different kind of customer-context: large organizations that needed help managing their private fleets. A final observation from the diagram is that Apple's iPod pops up as a capability-contributing business model once again. This illustrates the value-appropriating power of own a business model like Apple's that is useful to such a wide variety of firms.

Chapter 5
Using the VISOR Palette for Enterprise 2020: Scenarios and Configurations

In this chapter, we utilize the VISOR palette to analyze enterprises in the same industries whose example case we analyzed in Chap. 4, but projected for 2020.

Scenario planning is a disciplined method for imagining possible futures that generally companies have applied to a range of issues (Schoemaker 1995). Unlike traditional strategic planning, which usually assumes there is only one best solution to a strategic question, scenario planning entertains multiple possibilities (Garvin and Levesque 2006). The Royal Dutch-Shell corporation was one of the first companies to use this methodology since the early 1970 s, as part of it process of generating and evaluating strategic options (Schoemaker and van der Heijden 1992). Traditional scenario planning incorporates 10 components (Shoemaker 1995):

- Defining the scope: here, the time frame and scope of analyses in terms of markets, geographical areas, and technologies are established
- Identifying the major stakeholders: customers, suppliers, competitors, employees, share-holders, government and others who would be affected by or influence the issues are identified
- Identifying basic trends: what are the political, economic, societal, technological, legal and industry trends that may affect the issue under analysis
- Key uncertainties: identifies the uncertain outcomes or events that will significantly affect the issue being addressed
- Construction of initial scenario themes: developing an initial narrative that identifies extreme outcomes or some measures of clustering events
- Consistency and plausibility check: running internal consistency checks on trends, the outcome combinations and reaction of stakeholders
- Developing learning scenarios: extracting general themes and lessons from the initial scenarios developed
- Identifying research needs: engaging in future research to flesh out further understanding of uncertainties and themes

O. A. El Sawy and F. Pereira, *Business Modelling in the Dynamic Digital Space*, SpringerBriefs in Digital Spaces, DOI: 10.1007/978-3-642-31765-1_5,

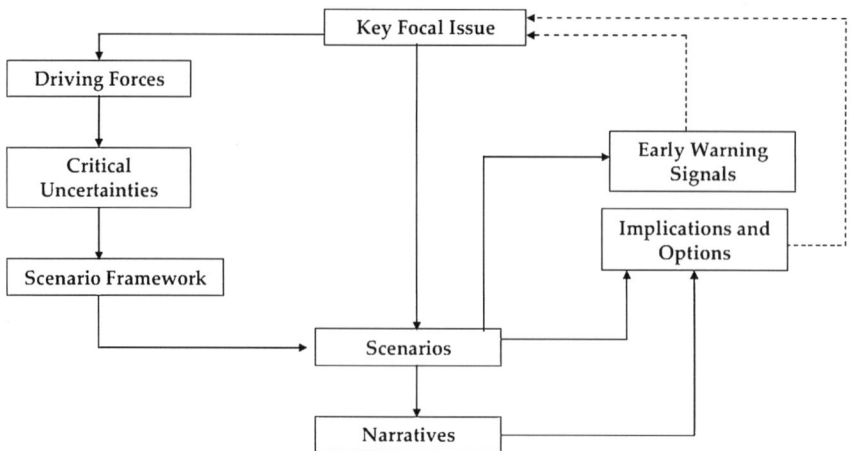

Fig. 5.1 Scenario planning components (Garvin and Levesque 2006)

- Developing quantitative methods: reexamining the internal consistencies of the scenarios to assess if quantitative models could be developed
- Evolution towards decision scenarios: adopting an iterative process to converge on scenarios that can be used to test strategies and new ideas.

Since then, several variations and adaptations of this general approach have been developed, two models of which are illustrated in Figs. 5.1 and 5.2, but the key components remain.

5.1 VISOR and Scenario Planning

In this section we adopt the traditional scenario approach, and use the VISOR framework to discuss the scenarios and the resulting narratives, as shown in Fig. 5.1. Here we assume the following scenarios have prevailed:

5.1.1 Driving Forces

- In 2020, three major societal shifts will have occurred: First, with distributed co-creation of value the boundaries of the enterprise will be much more porous and it will be more difficult to define where the enterprise ends and the other parts of the ecosystem begin. Second, open innovation will likely be a dominant mode of operations as new products and services need to come to market more quickly for diverse customers. Third, the notion of prosumption will take hold as consumers of services and products engage in their production through processes that we are already seeing in phenomena such as user-generated content

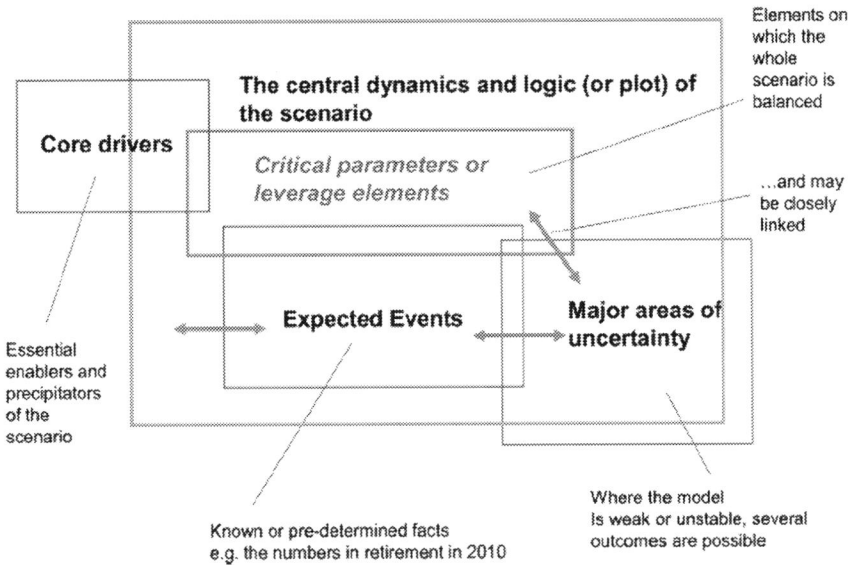

Fig. 5.2   Major building blocks for scenario construction (Forge et al. 2006)

- In 2020, the customer experience becomes primate as value is primarily created through the process of consumption and the experience which it creates. Designing more effective customer experiences around services provided through digital platforms will take center stage in designing new digital business models.

5.1.2   Critical Uncertainties

- In 2020, the proliferation of ubiquitous access, ease of capturing data, and digital services, will enable enterprises to engage in continuous sense-and-respond. Consequently, the launch of new products and services will be accompanied by digital online pilots that can cheaply and easily gather information. Thus new and emergent product testing will be done through online experiments in which products are tweaked and emerge continuously over time. Second, with all the burgeoning of sensor data, there will be a surge in sophistication in sensor data analytics that will enable intelligent interpretation of data.

With these "extreme positions" we articulate potential new digital business models that pivot around the various VISOR components to operationalize potential approaches to these new conditions. Such an exercise helps to derive new business model designs that would not otherwise be apparent. We call these extreme positions "yanks" as in yanking or pulling or tugging a rope with sudden force.

5.2 Extreme Yank 1: "Free, Perfect, Now" Digital Business Models in 2020

5.2.1 Scenario

In the digital ecosystem, regulations now allow for copies of digital products to be made without additional charges, both domestically and internationally. The World Trade Organization provides sanctions for violations. Intense competition by firms for similar digital products and consumer's un-willingness to pay for differentiation has led to firms offering the products for free. The ubiquitous access to digital products and service afforded by saturation of smart-phones, laptops, tables PCs and other mobile computing devices allows consumers to access all products instantaneously. These products, now because of their digital nature are "free from defects."

5.2.1.1 Narrative: Re-Configuring the Business Model

In this scenario, the traditional revenue model of the enterprise is disrupted, since firms cannot charge to deliver the value proposition to their customers. The enterprise has two options:

(i) Pivoting on the Interface: Charging for Levels of Access Experience

By 2020, with the multiplicity of modes of access, coupled with the maturity of technologies such as augmented reality and Light Emitting Diode (LED) paper, enterprises will be able to charge their customers for the levels of access experience they would want while consuming the digital product or service. These levels could include:

- Basic 2-dimensional access
- Interactive access
- Augmented reality access

Enterprises will be able to offer their customers personalized access when they consume the digital product or service. Table 5.1 explains how an enterprise will have to tweak its setting for the "Interface" component of VISOR if it intends to be successful in this approach (Fig. 5.3).

(ii) Pivoting on the Organizing Model

Enterprises will work with other enterprises in their value network which provide physical products and services to:

- Cross-sell: digital enterprises will provide their services free in exchange for customers to purchase physical goods from their partners. In general, this will entail a broad range of physical products that will complement the physical product
- Bundle: digital enterprises will bundle their digital products with physical products

Table 5.1 Configuring the four descriptors of the Interface in VISOR for "Free, Perfect, Now"

	Importance	Comments
Fluidity	★★★	Personalization and flexibility of access become relatively less important
Forgiveness	★★★★★	This becomes a key differentiator now among different enterprises. Any consumer or operator error must be redone instantaneously
Functionality	★★★★★	The ability to access range of services at different levels of experience become a major differentiator
Form factor	★★★	Still remains important, but not crucial for success of the approach

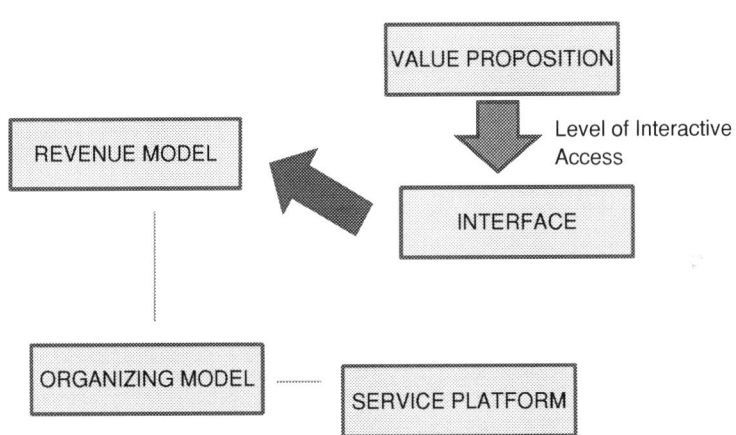

Fig. 5.3 Pivoting on Interface

- Third party access: digital enterprises will charge third parties for access to their customers

The service platform plays a vital role in seamlessly connecting the digital enterprise with all its partners to allow it to offer an integrated customer experience (Fig. 5.4).

Table 5.2 explains how, digital enterprises will have to tweak the settings of the Organizing model. In order to successfully execute on this new approach.

5.2.2 Re-Designing the Car Rental Enterprise for 2020

As discussed above in the ZipCar case study, the physical ownership and rental of assets, like cars, may not be necessary for an enterprise to generate value to its customers. In Table 5.3, we have suggested the "unthinkable" in that car rental agencies do not charge for the rental of cars in 2020 nor own cars as physical

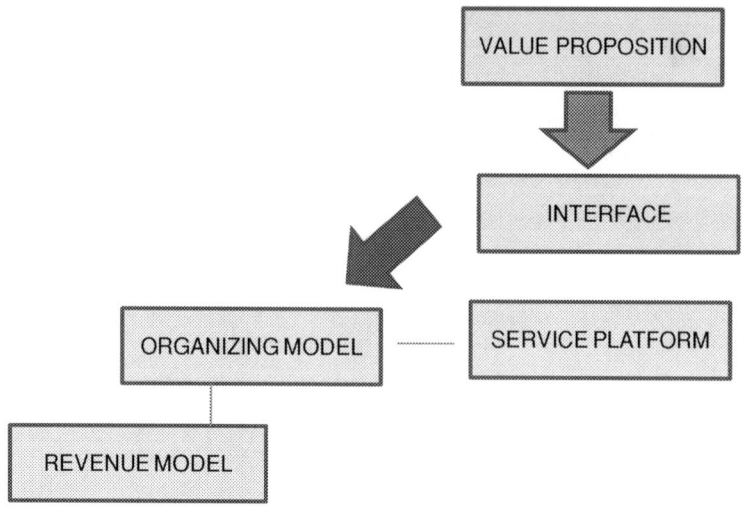

Fig. 5.4 Pivoting on the Organizing Model

Table 5.2 Configuring the 4-Ps of the organizing model in VISOR

	Importance	Action items
Processes	★★★	All processes must be fully automated
Partnerships	★★★★★	The digital enterprise must establish formal and long term partnerships to successfully execute on this approach
Pooling	★★★★★	Pooling of technology, products and services are vital to support bundling and cross-selling
Project management	★★★	

assets. The configurations in 2020 as illustrated in the table thus suggest an "obliteration" of the existing model as opposed to an incremental change. Car rental agencies will have to devise strategies of how to achieve the suggested configuration for 2020.

5.3 Extreme Yank 2: The Prosumption Model in 2020

5.3.1 Scenario

In the digital eco-system, consumers are now also creators of digital content that they can trade or sell over the network. Consumers may buy digital products from enterprises and add other features, which may then be resold (in a value-add

Table 5.3 Transforming the car rental enterprise for 2020

	Current configuration	Configuration in 2020
Value proposition	Daily rental of cars by mainly business travelers at transportation hubs, such as airports. Cars are assets owned by rental agencies	Free rental of cars from decentralized locations, on a membership basis. Cars are now and leased from various partners, such as corporations, government agencies, etc
Interface	Tele-phone or Internet reservation. Customer service is important	Multiple mode of access and virtual identification and authorization. AR allows keyless access to vehicle
Service platforms	Corporate intranet with limited access	Highly integrated and pooled with partners
Organizing model	Limited partnerships with some hotel chains and travel agencies	Formal alliances and intimate partnerships with Hotels, parking companies, government agencies etc
Revenue model	Daily car rentals and optional insurance	Cross-selling of other services

approach) and a portion returned to the enterprise in the form of royalty. Research and development of new features are crowd-sourced. Thus, open innovation is the norm and enterprises rely on consumers for improvements on existing digital products or new products. Enterprises sell to their consumers "basic" digital packages, which allow consumers to add different features for personal consumption and resale. This allows enterprises to lower their costs of production. Products are highly personalized and multiple variations exits. The traditional retail model is eliminated, and prosumers become agents for enterprises. Most enterprises are now small. This enables the "bottom of the pyramid" to be served.

5.3.1.1 Narrative: Re-Configuring the Business Model

In this scenario, the value-creation model of the firm is altered, and since value is now co-created with consumers, the traditional revenue model of the enterprise is altered. The enterprise will charge consumers a discounted cost of the initial digital product or service. In a sense prosumers become agents for the company. And so the corporate retail structure may also be affected.

(i) Pivoting on the Service Platform: Charging for Access to Partners

Enterprises will allow select prosumers to access their partners through controlled access to their service platform (Fig. 5.5). Table 5.4 explains how the enterprise's service platform has to be tweaked to support this new approach.

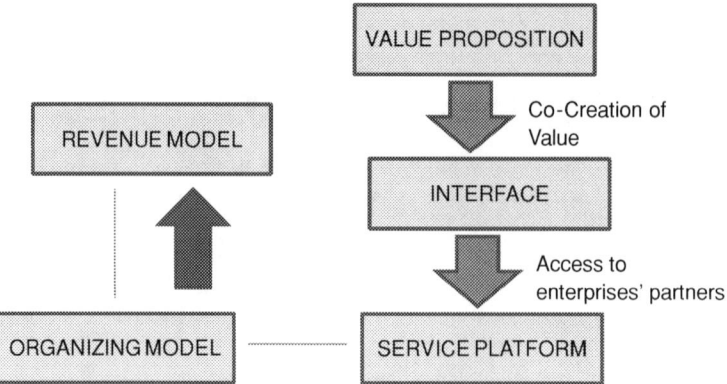

Fig. 5.5 Pivoting on the service platform

5.3.2 Transforming the Apparel Industry

Again, in Table 5.5, we have suggested the "unthinkable" in that manufacturers' of physical goods, such as sports apparel, allow their customers—prosumers—to customize and personalize their products. The configurations in 2020, as illustrated in the table, yet again suggest an "obliteration" of the existing model as opposed to an incremental change. The revenue model now would possibly revolve around digital monitoring services as opposed to the sale of the physical sport apparel.

5.4 Extreme Yank 3: "Real-Time Automated Improvisation" Digital Business Models in 2020

5.4.1 Scenario

In this scenario, the digital eco-system is characterized by proliferation of sensors, and the "Internet of Things" is fully realized. Massive data file analyses support real-time feedback, and mass opinion business intelligence is extensively used. This allows instantaneous experimentation and refinement of digital products and services.

In the health sector, "smart-pills" and skin-patch or "band-aid sensors are now widely deployed in patients. This allows for real-time diagnostics of effectiveness of dosage of medication, and automated re-adjustment.

Table 5.4 Configuring the four dimensions of Service Platform in VISOR

	Importance	
Access	★★★☆	Access to enterprise network and "partners" becomes important and is a differentiator
Agnostics	★★★★☆	Because it relies on open innovation and prosumers to develop and sell its products, the enterprise platform must support all operating systems
Architecture	★★★★☆	Enterprises will allow prosumer-agents to deliver their products across multiple platforms
Acquisition	★★	Enterprises will leverage existing infrastructures, as well as partners' networks

Table 5.5 Transforming the sports apparel industry

	Current configuration	Configuration in 2020
Value proposition	High quality, athletic footwear and apparel	Integrated digital and sensor technology to monitor body vital signs in athletic apparel. Apparel design are highly personalized, but body vital statistics monitoring is standardized
Interface	Store-front, possibly catalog and on-line ordering	Multi-modal and multi-sensory: Store-Front, Internet for online download sites, and mobile devices
Service platforms	Corporate intranet with limited access to partners	Optimized for consumers who have identified with the enterprise or "brand."
Organizing model	Traditional logistic-supply chain	Development of community of prosumers, identifying with enterprise brand, who provide multiple expertise on the network
Revenue model	Sale of footwear and athletic apparel	Revenues from health monitoring services, customer experience and royalties from re-sale of products

5.4.1.1 Narrative: Re-Configuring the Business Model

In this scenario, the traditional wellness and health-care sector is disrupted. The traditional doctor-patient paradigm is changed. Sensor technology allows diagnostics of potential medical problems analyzed against now pooled medical databases, and instantaneous tracking of changes in medical and health condition. Medical treatment is decentralized based on specific ailments or diseases, and smaller centers will arise. Supermarket-based Medical centers, such as Walmart and Carrefour are popular. Hospital care is for extreme and unanticipated emergencies like automobile or other types of accidents.

(i) Pivoting on the Organizing Model

Health Maintenance Organizations will work through these specialist centers, and reimburse for medical event avoidance. Enterprises will also reward employees for medical event avoidance. Table 5.6 suggests the tweaks that would be necessary for a successful execution of this new approach (Fig. 5.6).

Table 5.6 Configuring the 4-Ps of the Organizing Model in VISOR

	Importance	Action items
Processes	★★★★★	All processes must be fully automated
Partnerships	★★★★★	Formal partnerships are established between HMOs, and specialist centers
Pooling	★★★	Allow opportunities for partners to cross-sell medical services
Project management	★★★	Coordination of pooled offerings are important but automated processes will reduce pressure on human coordination

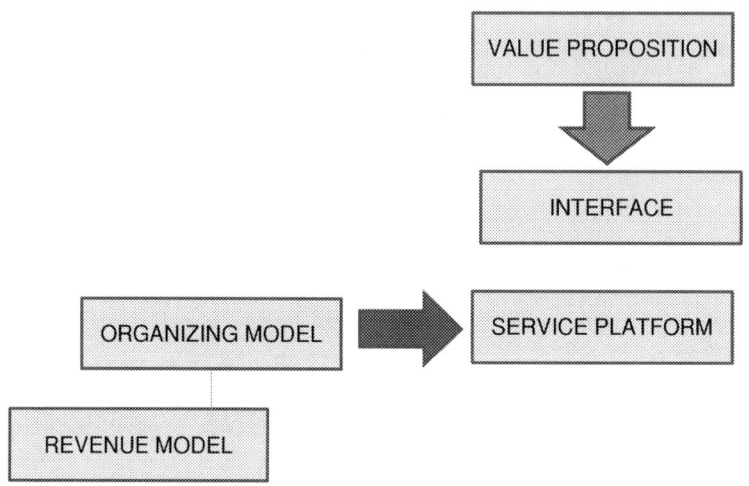

Fig. 5.6 Pivoting on the organizing model

Table 5.7 Transforming the Health Industry

	Current configuration	Configuration in 2020
Value	proposition	Health insurance and co-pay model
Enterprise will reward	employees for early detection and treatment	
Interface	Doctor-patient consultation	Sensor technology, body computing
Service platforms	Non-digital	Highly integrated with medical kiosks at shopping malls and work places
Organizing model	Limited to medical supply vendors	Partnerships with supermarkets, specialty medical centers, etc
Revenue model	Insurance premiums	Discounted insurance premiums plus employer rewards

5.4.2 *Transforming the Wellness and Health Industry*

Table 5.7, yet again, postulates an "unthinkable" scenario when Health Maintenance Organizations, Insures, and employers "pay" their subscribers for early
detection and medical event avoidance. The configurations in 2020, as illustrated
in the table, yet again suggest an "obliteration" of the existing model as opposed
to an incremental change. The revenue model now would possibly revolve around
prevention of catastrophic medical events and chronic disease incidences.

Conclusion and End Note

The scientific objective of this project has been to advance our conceptual understanding of the structure of business models for digital platforms by devising a unified modeling framework. This will allow us to better understand current and future business models, and to help the creation of a business model "what if" repository that researchers can continuously contribute to over time. This will also facilitate analyzing, from a more theoretical approach, the effects of disruptions and game changers. It will also allow a healthy interaction between research and practice in a way that advances both. Researchers will have a better common language and framework to communicate with, that will help them generate new types of business models. Finally, understanding business models that are in the midst of digital business ecosystems has deep societal influence on how we live and work.

We have refrained, in this study, from stereotyping or categorizing digital business models with categories such as long tail models or social network models or open innovation models, because there are infinite numbers of nuances and combinations and overlaps across them, and we have come to the conclusion that looking at VISOR configurations is a more helpful way to do that. The categorizations that we have seen so far are too vague to draw any insights from, and the we have found that the scenario generation and "yanks" have been more insightful and useful. The use of yanks and pivoting on different dimensions of the VISOR model has shown to be more fruitful in devising novel business models.

In conclusion, we want to highlight three important areas of opportunity for future research. First, a digital business model is not the same as a digital business strategy. An enterprise can have a wonderful digital business model, but if a competitor has a better one, then the enterprise is at a strategic disadvantage. Or, if the business model is not robust under environmental turbulence, then the enterprise is also at a strategic disadvantage. There is a need for further research to examine the linkages between the design of digital business models and strategic advantage. Second, systematic methods for the evolution of business models need

O. A. El Sawy and F. Pereira, *Business Modelling in the Dynamic Digital Space*,
SpringerBriefs in Digital Spaces, DOI: 10.1007/978-3-642-31765-1,
© The Author(s) 2013

to be developed. We have no good paradigms for the continuous redesign of digital business models and understanding when to make incremental changes or radical changes. Third, there is a fertile and socially rewarding area of research around digital business models that are focused on emerging economies and the bottom of the pyramid. Ultimately, it is to the disadvantaged in the world that digital business models with their leveraging potential will make the biggest societal difference.

SpringerBriefs on Digital Spaces

SpringerBriefs on Digital Spaces is an international research program—the ISD—launched in 2009 by the CIGREF Foundation (www.fondation-cigref.org). The series aims at making a set of concepts, ideas and results of projects carried out under the program available to the research, business and policy communities. ISD—Information Systems Dynamics, is a research program of public interest that works to evaluate the societal and managerial challenges related to the long-term use of information systems and digitality.

Since its launch in 2009, the program has already supported more than 30 projects conducted by international teams from different academic backgrounds (Computer Science, Management Science, Economics, Sociology, Geography and Anthropology) as well as from different geographical regions (Europe, North America and Asia).

The program works on the premise that the *spatial dimension* of the use of digital systems and artefacts is a critical perspective for understanding the dynamics of value creation—and more generally of socio-economizing—in our economies and societies. Understanding emerging practices in digital spaces is a key step toward delineating and conceptualizing a substantial part of the emerging paradigms of economic activities in the twenty-first century. *SpringerBriefs in Digital Spaces* publishes research findings and monographs related to the different facets of these issues. By doing so, the series seeks to contribute to the necessary dialogue between the researchers, practitioners and public policymakers involved in these very critical and rapidly changing fields of research and action.

Editor

The series is edited by Ahmed Bounfour, Professor, European Chair on Intellectual Capital Management, University Paris-Sud, and General Rapporteur of the ISD program.

O. A. El Sawy and F. Pereira, *Business Modelling in the Dynamic Digital Space*,　63
SpringerBriefs in Digital Spaces, DOI: 10.1007/978-3-642-31765-1,
© The Author(s) 2013

References

Afuah, A., & Tucci, C. (2001). *Internet business models and strategies*. New York: McGraw-Hill International Editions.

Al-Debei, M., & Avison, D. (2010). Developing a unified framework for the business model concept. *European Journal of Information System, 19*, 359–376.

Allee, V. (2000). Reconfiguring the value network. *Journal of Business Strategy, 21*, 1–6.

Baden-Fuller, C., Demil, B., Lecoq, X., & MacMillan, I. (2010). Editorial: Business models special issue. *Long Range Planning, 43*(2–3), 195–215.

Barney, J. (1991). Firm resources and sustained competitive advantage. *Journal of Management, 17*(1), 99.

Boland, R., Lyytinen, K., & Yoo, Y. (2007). Wakes of innovation in project networks: The case of digital 3-D representations in architecture, engineering, and construction. *Organization Science, 18*(4), 631–647.

Burgelman, R. A., & Grove, A. S. (2007). Cross-boundary disruptors: Powerful interindustry entrepreneurial change agents. *Strategic Entrepreneurship Journal, 1*(3–4), 315–327.

Casadesus-Masanell, R., & Ricart, J. (2009). From strategy to business models and tactics. Working Paper #10-036. Harvard Business School, November 2009.

Chesbrough, H. W. (2011). Bringing open innovation to services. *MIT Sloan Management Review, 52*(2), 85–90.

Chesbrough, H. W., & Appleyard, M. M. (2007). Open innovation and strategy. *California Management Review, 50*(1), 57–76.

Chesbrough, H., & Rosenbloom, R. S. (2001). *The role of the business model in capturing value from innovation: Evidence from XEROX corporation's technology spinoff companies*, Industrial and Corporate Change (submitted). Retrieved February 27, 2002, from http://www.hbs.edu/dor/papers2/0001/01-002.pdf

Demil, B., & Lecocq, X. (2010). Business model evolution: In search of dynamic consistency. *Long Range Planning, 43*(2–3), 227–246.

Dyer, J. H., & Singh, H. (1998). The relational view: Cooperative strategy and sources of interorganizational competitive advantage. *The Academy of Management Review, 23*(4), 660–679.

Eisenhardt, K., & Martin, J. (2000). Dynamic capabilities: What are they? *Strategic Management Journal, 21*, 1105–1121.

El Sawy, O. (2003). The IS Core IX: The 3 faces of IS identity: Connection, immersion, and fusion. *Communications of the Association for Information Systems, 12*(1), 588–598.

El Sawy, O. A., Malhotra, A., Gosain, S., & Young, K. M. (1999). IT-intensive value innovation in the electronic economy: Insights from marshall industries. *MIS Quarterly, 23*(3), 305–335.

O. A. El Sawy and F. Pereira, *Business Modelling in the Dynamic Digital Space*,
SpringerBriefs in Digital Spaces, DOI: 10.1007/978-3-642-31765-1,
© The Author(s) 2013

Emery, F. E., & Trist, E. L. (1965). The causal texture of organizational environments. *Human Relations, 18*(1), 21–32.

Fife, E., & Pereira, F. (2005). Adoption of mobile data services: Towards a framework for sector analysis. In P. Margherita (Ed.), *Mobile and wireless systems beyond 3G*. Pennsylvania: Idea Group.

Forge, S., Blackman, C., & Bohlin, E. (2006). Constructing and using scenarios to forecast demand for future mobile communication devices. *Foresight, 8*(3), 36–54.

Gavin, D., & Levesque, L. (2006). *A note on scenario planning*. Boston: Harvard Business School Publishing.

Gawer, A. (2009). *Platforms, markets and innovation* (1st ed.). Cheltenham, UK: Edward Elgar Publishing.

Gawer, A., & Cusumano, M. A. (2008). How companies become platform leaders. *MIT Sloan Management Review, 49*(2), 28–35.

Gordijn, J., Ostenwalder, A., & Piguer, Y. (2005). Comparing two business model ontologies for designing e-business models and value constellations. In *18th BLED Conference*, June 6–8, 2005. Bled, Slovenia.

Ho, Y. C., Fang, H. C., & Lin, J. F. (2010). Value co-creation in business models: Evidence from three case analyses in Taiwan. *The Business Review, 15*(2), 171–177.

Hoyer, V., & Stanoevska-Slabeva, K. (2009). Generic business model types for enterprise mashup intermediaries. In *Proceedings of the Fifteenth Americas Conference on Information Systems, San Francisco, California*, August 6–9, 2009.

Iansiti, M., & Levien, R. (2004). Strategy as ecology. *Harvard Business Review, 82*(3), 68–78.

Iyer, B., & Davenport, T. H. (2008). Reverse engineering Google's innovation machine. *Harvard Business Review, 86*(4), 58–68.

Johnson, M. W., Christensen, C. M., & Kagermann, H. (2008). Reinventing your business model. *Harvard Business Review, 86*(12), 50–59.

Lee, K. M., Yates, D. C., Joseph, W., & El Sawy, O. A. (2010). Value creation of mobile services through presence: Designing mobile information and entertainment applications with presence in mind. *Presence: Teleoperators and Virtual Environments, 19*(3), 265–279.

Leemhuis, J. P. (1985). Using scenarios to develop strategies. *Long Range Planning, 18*(2), 30–37.

Mageretta, J. (2002). Why business models matter. *Harvard Business Review, 80*(5), 86–92

Mahadevan, B. (2000). Business models for internet based E commerce: An anatomy. *California Management Review, 42*(4), 55–69.

Mayo, M. C., & Brown, G. S. (1999). Building a competitive business model. *Ivey Business Journal, 63*(3), 18.

Meyer, A. D., Gaba, V., & Colwell, K. A. (2005). Organizing far from equilibrium: Nonlinear change in organizational fields. *Organization Science, 16*(5), 456–473.

Morris, M., Schindehutte, M., & Allen, J. (2005). The entrepreneur's business model: Toward a unified perspective. *Journal of Business Research, 58*(6), 726–735.

Normann, R., & Ramírez, R. (1993). From value chain to value constellation: Designing interactive strategy. *Harvard Business Review, 71*(4), 65–77.

Osterwalder, A., & Pigneur, Y. (2009). *Business model generation: A handbook for visionaries, game changers, and challengers*. Hoboken: Wiley

Osterwalder, A., Pigneur, Y., & Tucci, C. (2005). Clarifying business models: Origins, present, and future of the concept. *Communications of the Association for Information Systems, 16*, 1–25.

Overby, E., Bharadwaj, A., & Sambamurthy, V. (2006). Enterprise agility and the enabling role of information technology. *European Journal of Information Systems, 15*(2), 120–131.

Pavlou, P. A., & El Sawy, O. A. (2010). The "third hand": IT-enabled competitive advantage in turbulence through improvisational capabilities. *Information Systems Research, 21*(3), 443–471.

Roland, M. Müller, R., Kijl, B., & Martens, J. (2011). A comparison of inter-organizational business models of mobile app stores: There is more than open vs. closed. *Journal of Theoretical and Applied Electronic Commerce Research, 6*(2), 63–76.

Sambamurthy, V., Bharadwaj, A., & Grover, V. (2003). Shaping agility through digital options: Reconceptualizing the role of information technology in contemporary firms. *MIS Quarterly, 27*(2), 237–263.

Schlagwein, D., & Schoder, D. (2011). *The management of open value creation.* Paper presented at the Hawaii International Conference on System Sciences.

Schlagwein, D., Schoder, D., & Fischbach, K. (2010). *An approach to an open resource-based view.* Paper presented at the Academy of Management (AOM).

Selsky, J. W., Goes, J., & Baburoglu, O. N. (2007). Contrasting perspectives of strategy making: Applications in 'hyper' environments. *Organization Studies, 28*(1), 71–94.

Shafer, S. M., Smith, H. J., & Linder, J. C. (2005). The power of business models. *Business Horizons, 48*(3), 199–207.

Shoemaker, P. (1995). Scenario planning: A tool for strategic thinking. *MIT Sloan Management Review, Winter, 36*(2), 25–40.

Shoemaker, P., & van der Heidjen, C. (1992). Integrating scenarios into strategic planning at the royal Dutch/Shell. *Strategy and Leadership, 20*(3), 41–46.

Slywotzky, A. J. (1996). *Value migration: How to think several moves ahead of the competition.* Boston: Harvard Business School Press.

Sorescu, A., Franbach, R., Singh, J., Rangaswamy, A., & Bridges, C. (2011). Innovations in retail business model. *Journal of Retailing, 87*(1), 3–16.

Stabell, C. B., & Fjeldstad, O. D. (1998). Configuring value for competitive advantage: On chains, shops, and networks. *Strategic Management Journal, 19*(5), 413–437.

Stewart, D. W., & Zhao, Q. (2000). Internet marketing, business models, and public policy: JPP&M JM & PP. *Journal of Public Policy and Marketing, 19*(2), 287.

Taleb, N. N. (2007). *The black swan: The impact of the highly improbable.* New York: Random House.

Teece, D. J. (1986). Profiting from technological innovation: Implications for integration, collaboration, licensing and public policy. *Research Policy, 15*(6), 285–305.

Teece, D. J. (2007). Explicating dynamic capabilities: The nature and microfoundations of (sustainable) enterprise performance. *Strategic Management Journal, 28*(13), 1319–1350.

Teece, D. J. (2010). Business models, business strategy and innovation. *Long Range Planning, 43*(2–3), 172–194.

Timmers, P. (2000). *Electronic commerce—strategies and models for business-to-business trading.* London: Wiley.

Vargo, S. L., & Lusch, R. F. (2004). Evolving to a new dominant logic for marketing. *Journal of Marketing, 68*(1), 1–17.

Vargo, S. L., & Lusch, R. F. (2008). Service-dominant logic: Continuing the evolution. *Journal of the Academy of Marketing Science, 36*(1), 1–10.

Wagner, C., & Majchrzak, A. (2007). Enabling customer-centricity using Wikis and the Wiki way. *Journal of Management Information Systems, 23*(3), 17–43.

Walls, J., Widmeyer, G., & El Sawy, O. (1992). Building information system design theory for vigilant EIS. *Information Systems Research, 3*(1), 36–59.

Walls, J., Widmeyer, G., & El Sawy, O. (2004). Assessing information system design theory in perspective: How useful was our 1192 initial rendition? *Journal of Information Technology Theory and Applications, 6*(2), 43–58.

West, J. (2003). How open is open enough?: Melding proprietary and open source platform strategies. *Research Policy, 32*(7), 1259–1285.

Winter, S. (2003). Understanding dynamic capabilities. *Strategic Management Journal, 24*(10), 991–995.

Workshop "digital challenges in innovation research". Retrieved from http://ssrn.com/abstract=1622170

Yoo, Y., Lyytinen, K. J., Boland, R. J., Jr., Berente, N., Gaskin, J., Schutz, D., et al. (2010). *The next wave of digital innovation: Opportunities and challenges: A report on the research workshop "digital challenges in innovation research"*. Retrieved from http://ssrn.com/abstract=1622170

Zott, C., & Amit, R. (2010). Business model design: An activity system perspective. *Long Range Planning, 43*, 216–226.